STARTUP GUIDE

#startupeverywhere

Startup Guide Los Angeles

EDITORIAL
Publisher: Sissel Hansen
Editor: Marissa van Uden
Proofreaders: Ted Hermann, Michelle Mills Smith
Staff Writers: Charmaine Li, L. Isaac Simon
Contributing Writers: Lily Karlin, Matthew Speiser, Michael Goitanich, Phineas Rueckert

PRODUCTION
Global Production Lead: Eglė Duleckytė
Local Project Manager: Allison Lubarsky
Researchers: Michael Kelly, Michael Goitanich, Ruxandra Nedelcu, Sofia Silva, Vera Oliveira
Local Ambassadors: Aria Cyrus Safar, Darlene Fukuji, John Diep, Kevin Winston, Krisztina 'Z' Holly

DESIGN & PHOTOGRAPHY
Designer: Cat Serafim
Photographers: Rachel McCarthy

Additional photography by Anna Andersen, Clay Larsen, Theresa Blank, Grey & Elle, Tom Lindboe, Art Center College, Coolhaus, 4YFN, Loyola Marymount University, Cal State LA, USC, Rachael Thompson, Janice Bryant Howroyd / The ActOne Group, Two Bit Circus, SAP Next-Gen, LA Kretz Innovation Campus and Unsplash.com

Illustrations by Joana Carvalho, Cat Serafim
Photo Editor: Daniela Carducci, Joana Carvalho

SALES & DISTRIBUTION
Global Partnerships Lead: Marlene do Vale marlene@startupguide.com
US Partnerships Lead: Allison Lubarsky allison@startupguide.com
Business Developer - APAC and Africa: Anna Weissensteiner anna@startupguide.com
Marketing Lead: Vera Oliveira vera@startupguide.com

Printed in Berlin, Germany by
Medialis-Offsetdruck GmbH
Heidelbergerstraße 65, 12435 Berlin

Published by Startup Guide World ApS
Kanonbådsvej 2, 1437 Copenhagen K

info@startupguide.com
Visit us: startupguide.com
@StartupGuideHQ

Worldwide distribution by Die Gestalten
Visit: gestalten.com

ISBN: 978-3-947624-13-3

STARTUP GUIDE
LOS ANGELES

STARTUP GUIDE LOS ANGELES

In partnership with The Los Angeles Coalition
for the Economy & Jobs

Proudly supported by

SAP next-gen ▶▶▎

BCG
Digital
Ventures

Early Growth
FINANCIAL SERVICES

Sissel Hansen
/ Startup Guide

Long known as the world's epicenter for arts and entertainment, Los Angeles is proving to be much more than that. In the past decade, LA has been nurturing a crop of creatives and entrepreneurs across industries who are keen on founding the businesses of tomorrow.

With the likes of Tinder, Hulu and SpaceX having their roots in California's biggest city, LA's startup ecosystem is developing rapidly and increasingly garnering attention on the international stage. According to the 2019 Global Startup Ecosystem report, LA climbed to spot #6 on the list of top startup ecosystems around the world, sharing its ranking with Tel Aviv. Additionally, the report showed that LA is one of the most dynamic cities in the US for gaming, adtech and life-sciences startups.

In addition to warm weather and vibrant nature, the city boasts world-class universities, such as Caltech, UCLA and USC, as well as a diverse talent pool that consists of a unique blend of creative and tech types. Not only that, a number of exciting startups aiming to leave a social impact have emerged. For instance, AppliedVR is creating virtual reality experiences with the goal of treating pain, anxiety or stress associated with physical illnesses, and The Female Quotient is aiming to promote equality in workplaces around the world.

One thing's clear: LA's startup scene is heating up. That's why Startup Guide Los Angeles features all the need-to-know resources, programs, spaces and tips for any entrepreneur looking to start up in the sunny city. It also features interviews with some of the founders and investors who have successfully challenged the historical dominance of Silicon Valley to establish their very own hub: "Silicon Beach."

Sissel Hansen
Founder and CEO of Startup Guide

Eric Garcetti
/ Mayor of Los Angeles

Dear Friends,

There's never been a better time to launch a startup in Los Angeles – a city defined by freedom, belonging and innovation; a city shaped by a tradition of creativity and a future full of promise; a city determined to remain a global crossroads of culture and commerce, and a center of dynamism, opportunity and prosperity for generations ahead.

Los Angeles is in the midst of a remarkable moment. We are taking big steps to confront the great challenges of our time: from climate change to education to economic inequality and more. We are building an economy today that will last and grow tomorrow – and long into the lives of our children and grandchildren.

We have a diverse population and the third-largest metropolitan economy on the planet. We've seen record venture capital investments flowing into our companies in the past five years. We have homegrown tech talent with more engineers graduating from local universities than any other area in the country, and we have a strong track record of attracting top students and the very best entrepreneurs from everywhere.

Our port is the busiest in the Western Hemisphere, a critical conduit between businesses at home and markets abroad. Our airport is the fifth-busiest in the world, a key gateway to people and places on distant shores. Our residents hail from more than 140 countries and speak upwards of two hundred languages. Our artists and entertainers are reimagining content and redefining our culture, and distributing it to domestic communities and on distant shores.

Perhaps most of all, our infrastructure is on the move – as we invest $120 billion in public transit, rail, roads and bridges, and we welcome a private sector testing hyperloops, dockless scooters, electric and autonomous vehicles, unmanned aerial vehicles, 5G and more on our streets and in our neighborhoods.

Simply put, Los Angeles is a city with the vision, determination, perseverance and persistence to succeed, just the qualities needed for any startup to get off the ground and thrive. We are ready to welcome you with open arms and show you what makes Los Angeles a home of possibility and an epicenter of opportunity.

Los Angeles Mayor Eric Garcetti

Local Community Partner / The Los Angeles Coalition for the Economy & Jobs

LA culture is startup culture.

LA is a trillion-dollar economy with an average of 329 days of sunshine a year and unparalleled attractions. Our startup community, home to Snap, Riot, SpaceX and Hulu, to name a few, is fueled from a deep pool of talent from coming from around the world and graduating from some of the region's 112 college and university campuses, which produce more PhDs and graduate degrees than any other city in America.

This talent development is being fueled by digital Hollywood's demand for storytellers, the growth of the aerospace industry into commercial markets, and the blue and green economies' quest for sustainable and planet-saving solutions.

LA's media giants and global cultural influencers are amplifying the impact of the region's digital makers and attracting tens of billions of investment dollars into its startup scene, making LA "ground zero" for launching new marketplace business models that attract the attention of the city's ten million plus residents, who represent more than 140 nationalities and speak more than 224 languages.

LA was and is built on vision and entrepreneurial spirit. No matter what your background, your opportunities to dream, collaborate and implement are limitless. When the workday is over, go to Silicon Beach for the surfing but stay to join the arts, culinary, entertainment and tech talent that gravitates here, shaping the global conversation from a taco truck, demo track, explosive video clip or freewheeling digital vision.

Technology and innovation are in LA's DNA. We invite you to explore this guide and bring your startup dreams here.

Michael H. Kelly
Executive Director
The Los Angeles Coalition for the Economy & Jobs

contents

STARTUP
GUIDE
LOS ANGELES

startups

programs

spaces

experts

founders

schools

investors

Local Ecosystem

- LA has over 200 museums, 10,000 restaurants, and hundreds of movie theatres.
- According to the Motion Picture Association of America, LA releases 400 to 500 movies per year.
- Crowdspring blog rated LA as its #2 city in the US for Startups and Entrepreneurs in 2019.
- In 2018, the Southern California tech industry raised nearly $6.4 billion.
- At least $35 billion has been invested in LA startups from outside the city over the last decade.
- The city has 490 entrepreneurs per 100,000 people.
- Since 2010, for every dollar under management locally, 7 dollars has been invested in LA startups.
- The virtual reality and augmented reality industry raised $2 billion in funding in 2018.
- The median post-money valuation for seed-round funding in LA is $8.8 million and $28 million for Series A funding.
- LA ranks 7th in American Cities with respect to Language Diversity.

[Notable Startups]

- Dollar Shave Club was acquired by Unilever for $1 billion in 2016.
- Snapchat went public in 2017 with a market capitalization of $33 billion.
- Oculus, the digital entertainment and VR company, was acquired by Facebook for $2 billion in 2014.
- Beats (by Dre) was acquired by Apple for $3 billion in 2014.
- Ring was acquired by Amazon for $1 billion in 2018
- Fair raised $435 million in a Series B round in 2018
- Bird, the escooter company founded in 2017, has raised $415 million over four rounds.
- Beyond Meat, the plant-based protein company, raised $50 million in October of 2018 with a total raise of $122 million.

Sources: amplify.la/latech, builtinla.com, Businessinsider.com, city-data.com/us-cities, Forbes.com, fred.stlouisfed.org, laweekly.com, Quora.com, worldpopulationreview.com

[City] # Los Angeles,
United States of America

[Statistics:] GDP: $1.044 trillion (2017)
Land Area: 503 mi² (1,300 km²)
Population of Los Angeles: 4 million
Population of Greater Los Angeles Area: 18 million
Foreign population: 39.7%
Number of tech companies: 4,902
Most-spoken Languages: English and Spanish

STARTUP
GUIDE
LOS ANGELES

Los Angeles County Museum of Art - Los Angeles

Intro to the City

Los Angeles, the largest city in "the Golden State," is a mosaic of people and cultures. While its physical stature matches the undeniable impression it makes on the world stage, it's also a world center of business, trade, entertainment, media, culture and technology. With outstanding universities and research institutions, a budding startup culture, and an undeniable quality of life, the city is an icon of American prosperity and a beacon of the American dream.

While it's well known as the mecca of entertainment, with beautiful beaches and awe-inspiring mountains, the city has also been undergoing a silent evolution into the tech industry. The maturation of the tech scene comes as no surprise when one key factor is considered: money. The city has the third largest GDP in the world with a $1-trillion-plus, and venture funding to LA-area startups has quietly exploded over the last five years, earning LA the nickname "Silicon Beach" (in 2018, LA-based startups received $4.2 billion in VC funding, ranking third nationwide).

What's more, it's a city with vision. It's rethinking the space age in the city that first launched it, and rethinking technology from the city that sent the first email. It's a place that constantly interrogates the possibility of tomorrow and makes strides to turn those possibilities into realities. Most importantly, LA is the land of dreams, where more than one of every two hundred people is an entrepreneur.

Before You Come

It's said that LA isn't just one city but a mosaic of six or seven cities, and indeed its sprawling neighborhoods each have a unique culture and aesthetic. Before arriving, consider whether you want to live near the ocean, the mountains, the downtown core, or the up-and-coming eastside. Health and wellness is a large part of the city's culture, so you may want to brush up on your yoga practice (and vegan recipes) before you arrive. If you're moving from outside of the US and plan to stay longer than three months, you'll need a visa before your arrival. Note that 38 percent of Angelinos speak Spanish as their primary language, so learning some Spanish will make your transition even smoother. While LA is a bustling city, the infrastructure for public transportation has been slow to keep up, so you'll probably need a car. However, it is also a very congested city, with residents spending an average of 102 hours per year in traffic.

Cost of Living

As the global interest and appeal to live in LA has steadily risen for decades, so has its cost of living. With a median household income of $55,909 and a per capita individual income of $27,749, LA ranks twelfth in the US in median household income. However, housing is definitely not cheap. You should be prepared to fork out upwards of $2,000 for a comfortable one-bedroom (the average is $2,721). To stretch your budget, look in areas outside of the norm. Instead of moving to Beverly Hills, Santa Monica or Silverlake, take a look at places like Thai Town, Downtown or Mar Vista. Living near public transportation will also allow you to avoid the major cost of a car, but it's not recommended if you'll need to travel to remote corners of the city that don't have access to public transportation.

Hollywood Sign, Hollywood Hills - Los Angeles

Santa Monica Pier during sunset, Los Angeles

Cultural Differences

The city of stars is no stranger to spiritualists, health gurus or vegans, with PETA rating LA the number-one vegan-friendly city in the US in 2018. Thousands flock to the city for its vegan food scene, which boasts more than 150 vegan and vegan-friendly establishments. The city's cultural composition is diverse, with Latinos at the forefront (47.5 percent). In many stores, restaurants and shops, Spanish takes precedence over English. Don't be intimidated by this. Angelinos are positive people who appreciate a good-faith effort to grasp the Spanish language. LA also comprises large Caucasian, Asian and African American populations, which is reflected in the culture, from music to food to the arts and entertainment. One unifying force that brings these cultures together is sports: the Greater Los Angeles Area is home to eleven major league professional teams.

Renting an Apartment

In LA, plenty of apartment buildings and private homes have been sectioned into apartments. Real estate agents are useful but not essential for finding an apartment. Don't be afraid to negotiate prices, as agents often have relationships with the buildings that they show and prices are not necessarily locked in. There are also coliving spaces such as PodShare, Starcity and Outsite, where residents can rent individual suites or shared suites with communal bathrooms, living rooms and kitchens for short-term leases. Reputable sites include **westsiderentals.com** and **radpad.com**. If you prefer a central location with good restaurants and entertainment nearby, look at Downtown and Midcity. For a seaside community, look at Venice, Marina Del Rey, Mar Vista and Santa Monica. For those into the arts, craft beer and artisanal coffee (the hipster scene), try Silverlake and Echo Park. Family-friendly areas include Playa Del Rey, Manhattan Beach and Pasadena. For that "boujee Hollywood" life, check out Beverly Hills and West Hollywood.

See **Flats and Rentals** page **194**

Walt Disney Concert Hall - Los Angeles

Insurance

Healthcare is constantly changing in the US, and California is no exception. If you're visiting the state and are not tied to an employer or university, you can purchase travelers insurance from a variety of providers, such as Kaiser Permanente, Aflac or AARP. For temporary travelers insurance, expect to pay in the range of $31 to $115 per week. For residents, health insurance is mandatory and can be expensive. However, if you're enrolled in school or employed within the state, you may be eligible for significant reductions or health benefits. A good starting point in searching for insurance quotes are aggregate services such as **healthcare.com** and **healthforcalifornia.com**, or check out California's official insurance marketplace at Covered California (**coveredca.com**). Insurance plans vary in cost and coverage, depending on your age, gender, medical history and income.

See **Insurance Companies** page **194**

Visas and Work Permits

How long you'd like to stay in the US determines which visa to apply for. For stays of longer than ninety days, you can apply for a variety of visas that last for up to three years. There are also permanent visas you can qualify for based on whether or not you have family in the US, your work experience, and whether or not you have plans to invest within the country. Some of the standard visas offered within the tech space are the H-1B, B-1, DS 160, and the T-N for non-immigrant Canadian and Mexican applicants. Another common visa for entrepreneurs is the E-2 Investor Visa, which allows you to enter and work in the US on the basis of an investment that you'll be controlling within the US. With all of these visas, you can live and work in the US for extended periods of time. You may also be eligible to apply for a Green Card to live and work in the US on a permanent basis, once the requirements of your visa have been fulfilled. Each visa has its own benefits and limitations. For example, the H-1B will tie you to a specific employer, whereas the B-1 Visa will allow you to pursue various work opportunities, but only for a period of six months and with the intent to return to your country of residence. Consulting with an immigration lawyer is strongly advised before making a petition for a US visa.

See **Important Government Offices** page **194**

Under DTLA - Los Angeles

Taxes

In addition to US federal taxes, you must pay California state taxes. As with federal taxes, your individual or corporate state tax rates vary according to your type of business and income bracket (a higher annual income is taxed at a higher percentage). The current self-employment tax rate in California is 15.3 percent, so with individual income tax and federal tax included, you should expect to put aside 30–35 percent of your income for your annual taxes. The window for filing annual taxes in the US is January 29 to April 17. Professional tax-filing companies such as H&R Block are available, and there are also online tax-preparation companies; for example, TaxSlayer Pro and TurboTax. The IRS also offers its own FreeFile service. Organizations such as Optima Tax Relief offer free tax consultations, and nonprofits such as Volunteer Income Tax Assistance Program (VITA) provides free tax help and preparation services to individuals who earn less than $65,000 per year.

See **Financial Services** page **193**

Starting a Company

The first step to starting a business in LA is to choose your company type – for-profit, nonprofit or limited liability (LLC). All companies doing business in the City of Los Angeles must register with the city and pay annual business taxes. Registering with the county, state and federal government may also be required, depending on your company type. Incorporating your business entity with the California Secretary of State is necessary if you choose to structure your business as a partnership, corporation or LLC. To obtain an employment identification number (EIN), businesses must register with the US Internal Revenue Service (IRS). Obtaining a California Sales Tax Certificate Number (also known as a Seller's Permit) will allow you to charge and submit sales taxes. Finally, if you have employees, you'll need to obtain a Payroll Tax Account Number with the State of California.

There are paid services such as Legal Zoom (**legalzoom.com**) or charitable organizations, such as Start Up Nation (**startupnation.com**) and My Own Business (**scu.edu/mobi**), that help entrepreneurs start businesses. Start Up Nation provides counselling services from a variety of experts and peers who have started their own businesses, and My Own Business is a nonprofit devoted to educating entrepreneurs on how to start and run a business. The Central California Small Business Development Center (SBDC) is another great resource that provides mentoring services and free consulting from business experts in areas such as planning and cash-flow management. It also offers free seminars and training tools online at **centralcasbdc.com**.

See **Programs** page **51**

Venice Beach and Boardwalk - Los Angeles

Opening a Bank Account

Major banks in LA include Chase, Wells Fargo, U.S. Bank, Capital One, and Discover. Most banks charge a service fee of $12 to $25 per month for checking or savings accounts, as well as a minimum deposit of $25. Some, such as Capital One, will allow you to open a bank account online in as little as five minutes. If you're a student, there are a variety of banks, such as Chase, that will waive or cut service fees significantly with proof of enrollment. To open a bank account in LA, you'll need your Social Security Number or Tax Identification Number, proof of home address, email address, funding method, and additional information for any joint account holder. Most banks will require proof of a foreign or local address in the form of a lease, utility bill or other mail, a passport, and a driver's license.

See **Banks** page **191**

Getting Around

Despite LA's status as an epicenter of technology, its transportation system is lacking and the city is one of the most congested in the world. If you must commute, try to avoid the hours of 7–9 AM and 4–7 PM. While the Metro subway system functions well, it's not an expansive network and you may need to rely on buses or other options to reach some neighborhoods. The Metro Trip Planner on **metro.net** is a helpful resource. Metro Express passes are $1.75 per trip, $7 for a day pass and $25 for a week pass. Uber and Lyft rideshare services are popular and affordable, and escooters and ebikes are ubiquitous. Buses and Amtrak trains run from Union Station to San Francisco and many other cities, and Los Angeles International Airport's connectivity to global cities makes LA one of the most attractive business locations in the world.

Phone and Internet

The largest telecom providers in the US are Verizon Wireless, Sprint, AT&T and T-Mobile, and generally you should expect to pay within the range of $40 to $120 a month for your phone plan. Some providers, such as T-Mobile, offer benefits such as unlimited roaming across North America, starting at $70 per month, which may be beneficial for people who travel regularly between these countries. While the "big four" providers are the most widely used, alternative providers have disrupted the market with simple pricing models, such as Google Fi's $20 per month flat fee for unlimited calls and texts, $10 per GB of data, and roaming without extra cost; or Virgin Mobile Beyond Talk, which offers a variety of plans, including unlimited text and data with 300 minutes of talk for $35/month. Other alternatives include Republic Wireless, Ting, Airvoice Wireless and Straight Talk Wireless, which don't require a contract.

Downtown Los Angeles restaurant - Los Angeles

Learning the Language

Some helpful local words to familiarize yourself with include "the Valley" (which always references the San Fernando Valley), "South Bay" (the general area south of LAX), "NOHO" (North Hollywood), "WEHO" (West Hollywood), and "the Pass" (Sepulveda Pass). "I'm stuck in the pass" means you're on the Interstate 405 highway or Sepulveda between Mulholland and Sunset. Some useful Spanish words are "Adios" (goodbye), "Buen dia" (have a good day), "Gracias" (thank you) and "de nada" (you're welcome). Brushing up on your Spanish before moving to LA is recommended but not essential. The majority of the population speaks English with ease, but Spanish proficiency can give you a leg up. Local institutions like UCLA and USC offer continuing education classes for new and novice Spanish speakers, with varying class times and pricing from $500 to $5,000. Smaller, more affordable language academies such as UNAM Los Angeles offer group classes, private lessons and conversation clubs where you can learn Spanish and meet new people.

See **Language Schools** page **195**

Meeting People

Angelinos are known around the world as friendly and accepting people, and the city offers plenty of networking events from meetups and workshops to happy hours. Try meetups like Momentus or Network After Work to meet like-minded folks in the tech space. Built In LA, an online community for startups and tech companies, is a great resource for jobs, news and events. KoreaTown Run Club is a growing network of runners and community leaders in the downtown core, and there are many hiking groups for getting out to explore nature. The city's coffee shops are brimming with creatives, and bustling neighborhoods such as Santa Monica, Echo Park, Silverlake and Atwater Village lay claim to some of the nation's most eclectic farmers markets. The nightlife in West Hollywood and Venice Beach is a surefire way to meet new people, and popular bars in the city center include Bru Haus, The Library Bar, and The Bigfoot Lounge. Sofar Sounds is a concert series that organizes intimate gigs in LA.

ups

[Name]
AppliedVR

[Elevator Pitch]
"We focus on developing and distributing immersive therapeutics that fundamentally reduce human suffering. We are initially developing products to treat pain and anxiety through our VR treatments, powered by bio-data and driven by AI."

[The Story]
Founded in 2015, AppliedVR is developing a digital health platform that utilizes therapeutic virtual reality to treat chronic- and acute-pain patients. The company was created by David Sackman (executive chairman and chief visionary officer), Matthew Stoudt (chief executive officer) and Josh Sackman (president). They came up with the idea while working at LRW, a global market-research firm. "While exploring new ways of collecting data and insights through virtual reality, we discovered over thirty years of academic research demonstrating the power of VR to impact attitudes, behaviors and health outcomes," says Josh.

AppliedVR spun off of LRW to apply what the founders had learned about VR and behavior change to develop VR-based healthcare solutions. To validate these solutions, Josh and his cofounders teamed up with healthcare practitioners and academics and ran research trials at Cedars-Sinai, Children's Hospital Los Angeles, George Washington University and the Mayo Clinic. With the message of "transforming healthcare through the power of pixels," AppliedVR now offers a digital library of clinically validated, immersive and interactive experiences. Along with what Josh calls a "new treatment modality," AppliedVR is also working on the delivery of VR therapeutics prescriptions via the world's first VR Pharmacy. "We envision a world where patients access these next-generation digital therapeutics in the hospital, at home or in the clinic," he says.

[Funding History]

Angel   External   Pre-Seed   Seed

To fund the company initially, AppliedVR participated in the Techstars Cedars-Sinai Healthcare Accelerator in 2016. The accelerator provided some early success, which allowed AppliedVR to since raise a seed round as well as a Series A round.

[Milestones]
- Publishing peer-reviewed papers, demonstrating our product's efficacy with research partners like Cedars-Sinai and Children's Hospital Los Angeles.
- Introducing VR to over thirty thousand patients in over two hundred hospitals in multiple countries.
- Conducting strategic research with top-tier health systems and payers, leading to commercial partnerships.
- Recruiting a best-in-class leadership team of digital health veterans.

[Links]   Web: **appliedvr.io** Facebook: **appliedvr** Twitter: **@AppliedVRhealth**

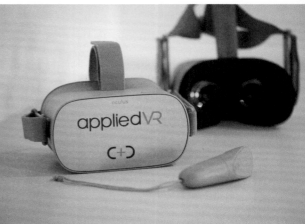

[Name]
Duuple

[Elevator Pitch]
"We developed an app that empowers individuals, brands and NGOs to create their own goal-based challenges. Through user-generated videos, users inject social good along with cheers, energy, excitement, prizes and sharing into people's daily lives."

[The Story]
Duuple, a unique social platform linked to charitable giving, was designed and launched in 2018 to encourage change. As a more personal and socially-conscious take on social media, Duuple invites people to share engaging photo and video content and then create challenges that act as fundraising sources for partnered charities, NGOs and other organizations. CEO Abby Frimpong, who was initially brought on by Duuple as a nonprofit expert and consultant, points to the ice bucket challenge as an inspiration for the app's philanthropic model of using technology to spread fundraising efforts in an energetic and viral way.

"At the heart of Duuple are tons of people inspiring community action for users to participate in exciting challenges and donating to causes and advocate for issues that matter," says Abby. "We intend to invite people to take action and give everyone an opportunity to become an agent of change." Since its creation, Duuple has seen how the simple act of social media posting can transform into a movement, especially when aligned with social initiatives. Individuals, brands and NGOs are choosing Duuple to create goal-based challenges to spread causes and calls-to-action because of the startup's strong dedication to honesty and fun. "The most important part of developing Duuple was to make it fun," says Abby. "We want people to be able to simply focus on fun and social good, to weed out the rest of the noise on social media."

[Funding History]

External   Pre-Seed   Seed

Unlike many app developers, Duuple did not bootstrap. Instead, the team held off on launching the app until 75 percent of the funds needed were raised. Duuple raised $1.8 million in its first round from private investors and another $1.8 million in a second round from lead venture capital investors Basel Holding.

[Milestones]
- Officially launching our app in the App Store.
- Welcoming our first user to the platform, who posted a selfie challenge.
- Partnering with Neil Patrick Harris and St. Jude Children's Research Hospital to do our first nonprofit challenge.
- Launching Duuple Asia with a kick-off event in Seoul, South Korea.

[Links]
Web: duuple.com Facebook: Duuple Twitter: @duuple Instagram: duuple

[Name]

Earny

[Elevator Pitch]

"We are a consumer-advocacy brand that helps consumers get money back."

[The Story]

By leveraging price protection, Earny works to make sure consumers never leave money on the table. The idea for the startup came after founder Oded Vakrat discovered the price-protection service offered by his Visa credit card, which provides buyers with refunds for the price difference of previously purchased items if the prices have since dropped. While the financial benefits of traditional price protection can be plentiful, the refunds are available only by request and the process to file a claim typically takes about forty-five minutes, rendering it unrealistic for most consumers to chase down all the available refund opportunities. Earny intervenes, acting as an intermediary by automating that process. Consumers connect their shopping and inbox accounts with the Earny service, which automatically monitors shopping activity. Customers can buy goods and services at listed prices, as Earny automatically alerts them to opportunities for price-protection refunds.

Earny began by automating retailer and credit-card price protection and recently partnered with Priceline to additionally offer hotel price protection. When customers book a reservation at a listed price that subsequently drops, Earny lets them know so they can rebook at the adjusted rate. As a consumer-advocacy brand, Earny prioritizes finding customers the best possible deals and giving back as much money as possible.

[Funding History]

Angel   External

To date, Earny has received $11.5 million in funding. At the seed stage, they received $2.5 million from Sweet Capital, Science Inc., Jeff Bonforte and Adam Nash. At Series A, they received $9 million from Science Inc., Comcast Ventures, Mayfield Fund and Oren Zeev.

[Milestones]

- Getting $10,000, $100,000, $1 million, then $10 million, etc., in refunds for customers.
- Attaining 10,000, 100,000 and then 1 million users.
- Expanding the team to 35 members.
- Raising a successful $9 million Series A round.
- Launching Earny Hotels price protection for travel.

[Links]   Web: **earny.co**   Facebook: **EarnyApp**   Twitter: **@earny**

[Name]

Fair

[Elevator Pitch]

"Buying a car should be simple and less costly than it is today. Technology can deliver that. We're focused on keeping people from having to go into debt to buy a depreciating asset when they can get access to the car they need on a month-to-month basis."

[The Story]

Fair was founded by Scott Painter and Georg Bauer, who are both passionate about using digital innovation to alleviate debt as a prerequisite of mobility. Their mission is to fundamentally disrupt how we access mobility and to prioritize fairness to customers. Rather than ask customers for the long-term commitment of a typical loan to purchase a car or a three-year car lease, Fair provides an alternative that fits into the millennial economic mindset and lifestyle. Users scan their driver's license, and, with a click of a button, they're pre-qualified for a monthly payment amount that fits their budget. Consumers use the car for as long they want and return it at any time. Every car comes with a limited warranty, roadside and routine maintenance, and an option for month-to-month car insurance.

Fair offers two program options: one for Uber drivers and one for personal use. Fair is Uber's exclusive partner for long-term vehicle solutions, so new drivers looking for a car are automatically directed to Fair. In under three years, the company has amassed a team of over four hundred employees and is steadily growing into new major cities.

[Funding History]

Seed   External

Fair has raised approximately half a billion dollars of equity capital to date and a little over a billion in debt. Investors include Softbank (an anchor investor) as well as car companies such as BMW and Mercedes.

[Milestones]

- Launching the company in August 2017.
- Acquiring Uber's Xchange Leasing Business in 2018.
- Hitting the mark of over one hundred deals a day.
- Raising over $500 million in equity in a year.

[Links]   Web: **fair.com** Facebook: **fairtheapp** Twitter: **@FairTheApp** Instagram: **fairtheapp**

[Name] # The Female Quotient

[Elevator Pitch] *"The Female Quotient is advancing equality in the workplace through collaboration, activating solutions for change and creating measurements for accountability. When you put women in any equation, there is a return on equality."*

[The Story] While preparing to attend the Consumer Electronics Show in Las Vegas in 2015, Shelley Zalis heard an interesting statistic: of the 150,000 people who attend CES each year, only 3 percent are women. Shelley didn't think that was right, so she told a few girlfriends, who told a few other girlfriends, and soon she had a group of fifty women attending CES with her. "Everyone's head turned when we showed up," Shelley said. "More business was done by women in those few days than ever before at CES."

This became the flashpoint for The Female Quotient (FQ), a business that strives to foster equality in workplaces around the world. The FQ accomplishes this goal through the realization of its three pillars: The first pillar is the FQ Lounge, a popup space at conferences and trade shows where women connect, collaborate and activate change together. The second pillar is the FQ practice, a consulting service helping businesses foster equality through bespoke bootcamps, machine learning, data analytics and tailored research. The third pillar is the FQ purpose, the philanthropic arm of The FQ that sells clothing and jewelry and donates the proceeds to nonprofits that support women. "Our goal is to have every company hold themselves accountable by closing the wage and diversity gap and allowing women to rise to leadership roles and thrive," Shelley says.

[Funding History]

Bootstrap

The Female Quotient has been bootstrapped from day one, using Shelley Zalis's personal funds. Today, The Female Quotient employs over twenty staff and is self-sufficient and profitable.

[Milestones]
- Creating an industry-collaborative mission where companies are working together to activate change.
- Creating a gender-equality score, which is now an industry standard.
- Fostering the largest global community of corporate women supporting one another.
- Building a brand that is anywhere and everywhere, connecting women, connecting leadership and activating change in the workplace.

[Links] Web: **thefemalequotient.com** Facebook: **FemaleQuotient** Twitter: **@femalequotient**

[Name]
NEXT Trucking

[Elevator Pitch]
"We're the first smart-trucking marketplace that connects shippers with carriers. Our technology is transforming the way shippers and truckers engage and communicate by creating an on-demand platform where shippers can instantly find truckers with capacity."

[The Story]
Four years ago, when entrepreneur Lidia Yan was starting to build her smart-shipping marketplace and bootstrapping with family money, she could have easily given up. As a woman founder with a background in communications, she had to confront skepticism at every turn. "It was a challenge when I wanted to raise money for a trucking startup because my background and experience didn't really align with what venture capitalists were looking for," Lidia says.

She was convinced nonetheless that she had the right idea, and that she was in the best place to pursue that idea. She teamed up with her husband, Elton Chung, to found NEXT Trucking. The company's success since has been impressive: the company now serves sixteen thousand drivers and has moved more than $50 billion worth of cargo. Its rapid growth has been as much about location as about timing. Forty percent of all merchandise that enters the US comes through the LA and Long Beach ports. Lidia saw a gap in the first mile of delivery services and used her own particular background to fill it. "Because of my family background in logistics, I understood what the industry is looking for, I understood what the driver is looking for, and we were confident that we were building a product that was really serving the industry and helping people change their lives."

[Funding History]

Bootstrap   External   Pre-Seed   Seed

NEXT Trucking began through bootstrapping. The company then raised a $2 million seed round and $5 million Series A round in 2016. In 2018, Sequoia Ventures led a $21 million Series B round. This year, NEXT Trucking cleared a $97 million Series C round led by Brookfield.

[Milestones]
- Launching its first app for truckers in 2016.
- Lidia winning Stevie Awards for women in business in consecutive years.
- Expanding the drayage facilities with eighteen acres in Long Beach, California.
- Being recognized as Forbes' Next Billion-Dollar Startup.

[Links]   Web: nexttrucking.com   Facebook: nexttrucking   Twitter: @nexttrucking   Instagram: nexttrucking

[Name] # Relativity Space

[Elevator Pitch] *"Relativity is building the first autonomous platform to build the future of humanity in space. Our long-term mission is to 3D print the first rocket made on Mars and help make humanity an interplanetary society."*

[The Story] Relativity Space uses 3D printing to radically alter the rocket-manufacturing process. From its inception, the company has focused on hardware development, creating a printer that will transform the creation of Earth-circulating satellites and eventually have the capacity to self-operate on Mars. Before founding Relativity Space, Jordan Noone and Tim Ellis had both worked on 3D printing in the private space sector and knew most companies were printing less than 1 percent of their rockets. Sharing a vision of the technology as integral to the future of rocket-building, they founded Relativity Space with the plan to raise that percentage to 95.

In the short term, the company's initial go-to-market products are 3D-printed rockets to launch satellites around Earth. This technology transfers to their long-term goal of 3D printing the first rocket on Mars and helping to create an interplanetary society. Relativity Space disrupts the traditional rocket-manufacturing modes with a drastic increase in efficiency, offering a simplified supply chain. Traditional rockets have approximately one hundred times the number of parts as 3D-printed rockets and longer build times. Traditional rockets take up to eighteen months to build, but Relativity Space hopes to take rockets from raw material to flight in a period of sixty days. 3D-printed rockets also mean a shorter iteration cycle, as automation capabilities allow for a change of rocket design every six months.

[Funding History]

Angel

External

Seed

Relativity Space has raised $45 million to date. After cold emailing Mark Cuban, the founders received a response within five minutes that he would fund their entire seed round. They were also accepted into the accelerator Y Combinator, which led to raising an additional $10 million for Series A.

[Milestones]
- Announcing our first three commercial customers.
- Becoming the first venture-backed company to win approval for a site at Cape Canaveral Air Force Base.
- Partnering with NASA's Stennis Space Center to build the world's first autonomous rocket factory.
- CEO Tim Ellis joining the National Space Council Users Advisory Group as the youngest member by twenty years.

[Links] Web: v Facebook: **relativityspace** Twitter: **@relativityspace**

Wondery

[Name]

[Elevator Pitch]

"We're the largest independent podcast publisher in the US. We're known for immersive storytelling podcasts like Dr. Death, Gladiator, Dirty John and Business Wars."

[The Story]

Around 2016, Hernan Lopez began to notice something: people would not stop talking about podcasts. Curious, Hernan – who, at the time, was president of Fox Network's international channels – began to investigate. "Any time you find a passionate group of early adopters, you have to learn why they like what they like so much, and determine if its growth is constrained by supply or demand," he says. What he found intrigued him: the podcast space was booming, but many of them sounded alike. He believed he could address a market inefficiency by creating immersive podcasts that make listeners feel like they're in the story. Thus, Wondery was born.

Hernan assembled a small team and began working to help podcasters increase their audience and monetize their shows. At the same time, they began looking for podcasts to produce. In 2017, they partnered with The Los Angeles Times to create the podcast Dirty John, about a real-life con artist. The podcast was downloaded over ten million times within six weeks of release. They found more success with podcasts such as Dr. Death and Gladiator. In 2018, Wondery raised $5 million in a Series A investment round. The team has now grown to over thirty people, and Hernan only sees it getting bigger. "There is a big growth trajectory in the podcast space and we see Wondery leading the way."

[Funding History]

Bootstrap

External

Seed

Hernan Lopez launched Wondery with his own money and investments from friends and family. He managed to bootstrap until 2018, when Greycroft and Lerer Hippeau led a $5 million Series A investment round in Wondery.

[Milestones]

- Partnering with The Los Angeles Times to produce the extremely popular podcast Dirty John.
- Following up this success with other popular podcasts, which helped us get the momentum to raise a Series A.
- Having Dirty John, Gladiator, and Dr. Death spend a combined 91 days on top of the iTunes most-downloaded-podcast charts.
- Becoming a top-three podcast publisher in September 2018 in terms of monthly audience.

[Links]   Web: wondery.com Facebook: wonderymedia Twitter: @Wondery

rams

In partnership with:

- **Be committed.**
  We seek to work with founders who have demonstrated a commitment to their goal, whether through hiring team members, customer discovery or taking initial steps towards the launch process.

- **Demonstrate coachability.**
  We look for applicants, regardless of stage or industry, who are open to feedback and can specifically benefit from the program's advising expertise and mentorship opportunities.

- **Connect on a personal level.**
  It's one thing to evaluate a startup on paper; it's another to talk to a human being. We speak to our applicants in a phone-interview process to make sure our advisers and founders connect and match on a personal level, in addition to matching company challenges to advisor strengths.

- **Have a clear vision.**
  We're interested in working with founders who have a clear understanding of why they're starting their company and what problem they hope to solve.

[Name] # Bixel Exchange

[Elevator Pitch] *"We recognize talent is equally distributed and opportunity is not. We empower all tech entrepreneurs to sustainably launch and scale their companies."*

[Sector] **Tech**

[Description] Bixel Exchange strives to create a startup community in LA that actually reflects the true makeup of the city. A collaboration between the Los Angeles Area Chamber of Commerce and the Los Angeles Small Business Development Center Network, it operates as a nonprofit focused specifically on diversifying representation in the city's emerging tech sector, a field that has historically skewed disproportionately white and male. Both industry and stage agnostic, Bixel Exchange nurtures emerging talent with two signature programs: Startup LAunch, which helps grow emerging startups; and Tech Talent Pipeline Program, which provides opportunities for underprivileged high school and college students to enter the tech industry. Providing a much-needed service to the city's developing industry is the primary goal: both programs are offered free of charge to participants with no equity participation.

The Startup LAunch program focuses on diversifying entrepreneurs building startups in LA, creating a generation of founders that accurately mirrors the diversity of the city. Aside from its zero-cost, no-equity model, it stands out from other incubation programs due to its mentorship focus of over thirty-five core advisors who represent the diversity in Los Angeles, as well as tailored program experiences and one-on-one advising opportunities. The program provides guidance on every step of the startup launch process, from fundraising to building a financial model, marketing and business strategy. It works to connect LA residents outside the insular startup bubble to venture capital firms and other investment opportunities necessary to successfully launch and prosper. The Tech Talent Pipeline Program helps underserved high school and community college students launch careers in the tech industry through work with the Mayor of Los Angeles and over sixty tech companies. Last year, the program placed two hundred community college students at sixty different tech companies, none of which had ever hired community college graduates before due to the stigma against community college (as opposed to four-year college) that typically hinders those not born into privilege from breaking into the startup industry.

[Apply to] bixelexchange@lachamber.com

[Links] Web: bixelexchange.com Facebook: BixelExchange Twitter: @BixelExchange Instagram: bixelexchange

- **Know your mission.**
  Startups should clearly articulate the problem
  their product or service solves. Long theoretical
  paragraphs aren't necessary; companies with
  strong potential can succinctly and effectively
  convey their strengths.

- **Understand your sphere.**
  Demonstrate commitment to understanding
  the space your company inhabits. Passion for
  the problems you're working to solve translates
  into connected and effective solutions..

- **Answer the why.**
  Founders should be able to communicate answers
  to "Why you?" and "Why now?" Be able to spell out
  to interested parties the vital resource your company
  will provide.

- **Offer something different.**
  Uniqueness is vital. Whether offering an entirely
  new resource or an innovative solution to a common
  problem, articulating your unique value proposition
  is key to being competitive in the market.

[Name]
Grid110

[Elevator Pitch]
"Our goal is to help entrepreneurs realize sustainable growth paths. We focus on activating community with the intention that the companies we work with will reinvest back into their local areas. We create opportunity through access to resources and revitalize cities through entrepreneurship."

[Sector]
Vertical agnostic

[Description]
Grid110 provides access to office space, community and resources to both tech and non-tech entrepreneurs through two accelerator programs. The nonprofit, which is grant-funded and partnered with the Mayor of Los Angeles, began as a way to activate Downtown Los Angeles as the next regional startup hub and to provide resources that weren't otherwise readily available to the area. The seven entrepreneurs that made up Grid110's founding collective partnered with real-estate companies looking to bring occupants into available buildings in the area. They appealed to smaller companies through an incubator program – now known as the Residency Program – that provides vital resources and mentoring opportunities to develop post-prototype startups. After receiving an influx of applications from earlier stage startups, Grid110 added its second, more-structured program aimed at initial founding steps: the Idea to Prototype program.

The Residency Program facilitates the growth process of five to seven already-established companies. Through weekly group sessions, private mentoring opportunities and access to the Grid110 network, teams focus on strengthening the efficacy of their businesses through reaching key milestones.

The Idea to Prototype program helps entrepreneurs at the initial stages of the founding process, with its opportunities for connections among companies proving one of its greatest draws. Meeting two nights a week – ideal for founders still making their living from full-time day jobs – the eight-week program helps companies work toward milestones related to value proposition, customer discovery, branding and product development. Founders learn how to home in on an extremely specific problem their company will solve and to be flexible and listen to potential opportunities for change in early stages. Each participant completes the program with a ready-to-use, two-minute pitch. The nonprofit neither charges nor takes company equity from program participants, and more than 65 percent of participating companies are led by founders from traditionally underrepresented backgrounds.

[Apply to]
grid110.org

[Links]
Web: **grid110.org** Facebook: **grid110** Twitter: **@GRID110** Instagram: **grid110**

- **Create products with a large market opportunity.**
  In your application, demonstrate the way your business will fundamentally alter its sector.

- **Have a clear track towards scalability.**
  We look for companies who can realistically manufacture their product at high volume.

- **Be curious.**
  The accelerator program floods founders with potential resources. We look for founders who can navigate their way through these opportunities through curiosity and by asking pointed, challenging questions.

- **Work within an emerging market.**
  We believe Southern California has a leg up in certain emerging sectors. We favor companies working within those fields or markets, which include food and agtech, mobility, aerospace, medical devices, advanced manufacturing, industry 4.0, biotech, new materials, cleantech and Latin America.

[Name]	# MiLA

[Elevator Pitch]

"We help entrepreneurs go from a prototype to a business. Our accelerator empowers entrepreneurs and their business by making hardware not hard. We accept seed-stage companies, cultivate innovation and groom for execution."

[Sector]

Hardware

[Description]

Make in LA (MiLA), the accelerator program of VC firm MiLA Capital, was created to fill a gap in hardware entrepreneurship in the LA startup scene. With both manufacturing and finance expertise, founders Shaun Arora, Noramay Cadena and Carmen Palafox were aware of the region's strong pool of manufacturing talent and saw how it could work in tandem with hardware founders to bring innovations to market. The MiLA accelerator nurtures emerging hardware founders through an application-based four-month program in Los Angeles and also provides funding (via MiLA Capital) for the accepted entrepreneurs. The program is designed to help founders move swiftly and efficiently to the next stage of their enterprise, providing targeted assistance in steps related to the business model, go-to-market strategy, prototyping and manufacturing. Participating startups receive an initial investment of $100,000 and have the opportunity to meet investors throughout the program. The program tests for pain points in each startup's business model and offers guidance on manufacturability and determining customer base. Cohort size is relatively small at five to seven, enabling a dedicated focus on each company.

Startups invited to join the MiLA program also benefit from access to coworking space and community. The accelerator is housed within the greater innovation lab Toolbox LA, which includes coworking, event and maker spaces and a biotech lab. Founders can also participate in networking events to connect with key players in the LA startup scene and receive advice during their own work process through one-on-one office-hour sessions with MiLA.

One company that went through the accelerator program is Amped Innovation, which MiLA cites as evidence against the myth that hardware companies are prohibitively capital-intensive and slow to market. Amped Innovation designs renewable energy products that have the ability to generate income – for example, a maize grinder that then allows for food production – and it has an intended customer base of those with an income of under $4 a day. It was founded in 2016 and went to market the following year.

[Apply to]

makeinla.com/apply

[Links]

Web: **makeinla.com** Facebook: **makeinla** Twitter: **@MakeinLA** Instagram: **make_in_la**

- **Have a singular vision.**
  We strive to work with companies that have unique insights into their field. Be able to answer this question: Why are you the only person who could – and should – launch this company?

- **Shake it up.**
  We're interested in partnering with founders changing their sphere of interest, whether creating something totally new or redefining an existing business.

- **Appeal to a large market.**
  Do you have a fresh point of entry into a major field? We love working alongside companies that could alter a fundamental function of society. How will your company change the way we live on a day-to-day basis?

- **Have an equipped team.**
  We invest, first and foremost, in the people behind a business dedicated to a heads-down approach to taking their product to market. Are you and your team ready for the challenge?

MuckerLab

[Name]

[Elevator Pitch]
"We are a low-volume, high-touch accelerator that works with a small number of companies over the course of a year or more on go-to-market strategy and company building. No three-month bootcamps. No demo days."

[Sector]
Enterprise software, marketplaces, consumer services

[Description]
MuckerLab provides founders with access to resources, funding and an extensive mentor network, ensuring that each and every company achieves the operating milestones required for the next round of financing. As Los Angeles emerged as an entrepreneurial tech hub, the team behind MuckerLab identified a gap that needed to be filled in the incubator and accelerator space. In a city with graduates from Caltech, USC and UCLA, as well as a host of already existing startups, MuckerLab strived to help nurture emerging talent into market-defining founders. The accelerator program stands out for its intimate nature: each year, it works with only ten to twelve companies early in their life cycle (at pre-seed or seed stage).

MuckerLab seeks founders working primarily on developing enterprise software, marketplaces and consumer services. Participating companies have the opportunity to work from MuckerLab's office and receive personalized guidance to take their enterprises to the next phase of development, starting with the fundamentals of product-market fit and then scaling. They also receive perks such as free cloud infrastructure and access to a large network of advisers and mentors. The final key component to the program is capital, with MuckerLab investing between $100,000 and $200,000 into every participating company.

Recent participants in MuckerLab include ServiceTitan, a software company for trade-industry services, such as plumbing and electrical contractors, that streamlines the way home-service entrepreneurs can run their businesses; and The Black Tux, which has reinvented the tuxedo rental process by allowing users to put their measurements into the website and get a tuxedo sent directly without going through the laborious in-person fitting process. In addition to their new venture incubation, MuckerLab also works with existing businesses to rework their core strategies or help specific departments spin off into their own startups.

[Apply to]
mucker.com/muckerlab-accelerator

[Links]
Web: **mucker.com/muckerlab-accelerator** Facebook: **MuckerCapital** Twitter: **@mucker**

- **Innovate with purpose.**
  Your innovations should be in the service of purpose and the SDGs. You should choose one or multiple SDGs in the development of your innovation and company as a guiding framework toward purpose and action to accelerate solutions toward the Global Goals.

- **Leverage exponential technologies.**
  Entrepreneurs and startups interested in connecting with the SAP Next-Gen global network should leverage exponential technologies and combine experience data with operational data to deliver insights leading to world-class experiences.

- **Don't be shy about your ideas.**
  As a member of the LA ecosystem, you should embrace the creativity of the city. You should unleash imagination through science-fiction thinking to unlock the purpose and potential impact of your innovations.

[Name]

SAP Next-Gen

[Elevator Pitch]

"We are a purpose-driven innovation university and community, enabling entrepreneurs and startups to connect with corporates, partners and academia and inspire innovation and experiences that accelerate solutions to the UN Sustainable Development Goals."

[Sector]

Media, cleantech, healthtech, climate action, utilities, smart cities and governments, academia, aerospace, entertainment, edutainment

[Description]

SAP Next-Gen is a purpose-driven innovation university and community aligned with SAP's commitment to the seventeen UN Sustainable Development Goals (SDGs). The SAP Next-Gen ecosystem includes a global network of educational institutions, labs, hubs, partners and NGOs, as well as innovation communities that help entrepreneurs and startups forge meaningful relationships with SAP's customer and partner base. SAP Next-Gen enables corporates to seed in disruptive innovation and co-innovate new experiences with startups to both create new business value and scale impact for the SDGs. Local entrepreneurs and startups are encouraged to get involved at the HanaHaus at Newport Beach, which shares a building with the SAP Innovation Center Network.

SAP Next-Gen services include global goals houses, living rooms and neighborhoods, innovation tours, meetups, boot-camps, industry summits, matchmaking between startups and corporates as well as advising and projects within academia. Sandra Moerch-Petersen, chief content director for SAP Next-Gen, says, "We are driving an innovation-with-purpose movement, uniting an open community of change-makers implementing the SDGs as part of their startup ideas and solutions through tech and innovation." SAP Next-Gen offers member startups, corporates and citizens a community with which to connect, team up and scale. "It's often about having the right network, and we believe in open systems and providing access," says Sandra.

One of the defining characteristics of LA's innovation ecosystem is its abundant creativity. "LA is one of the world's leading centers for storytelling arts," says Ben Christensen, the global lead for the SAP Next-Gen science-fiction thinking community. Both Sandra and Ben advise startups to leverage creativity and the arts and to unlock their imaginations with science-fiction thinking to accelerate progress towards the UN SDGs. "For SAP Next-Gen's communities of purpose and innovation, science-fiction thinking is an essential creative thread in the forward-looking ecosystem of LA," says Ben. Adventurous innovators with purpose-driven mindsets can find a home in SAP Next-Gen's LA and global networks.

[Apply to]

sapnextgen@sap.com

[Links]

Web: **sap.com/next-gen** Facebook: **SAPNextGen** Twitter: **@SAPNextGen** Instagram: **sapnextgen**

- **Have a strong team.**
  We look for companies that have a strong team of leaders in place for fruitful and dynamic collaboration.

- **Demonstrate awareness of growth areas.**
  We seek companies with an awareness of growth areas in the market space. Are you innovating in an area of burgeoning interest and creation? Can you help take emerging technologies to their next phase of development?

- **Apply aerospace to another market.**
  We work with companies applying aerospace technology to other markets, such as drone technology for telecommunications or geospatial imagery as an agricultural tool.

- **Create enabling tech for the aerospace industry.**
  We also work with companies in fields like energy management, block chain, robotics and artificial intelligence that are creating enabling tech for the aerospace industry.

[Name]
Starburst Accelerator

[Elevator Pitch]
"Helping startups grow in aerospace. Helping aviation, space and defense industries embrace open innovation and product development with startups."

[Sector]
Aerospace (aviation, space, defense)

[Description]
An innovation catalyst in the aerospace industry and the first global aerospace accelerator, Starburst matches corporates with startups while providing strategic-growth consulting for startups and corporations alike. With offices in Los Angeles, San Francisco, Montreal, Paris, Munich, Abu Dhabi and Singapore, the team has built an international ecosystem of key players across the aerospace industry, including over four thousand related startups. Every year Starburst hosts numerous national and international events, bringing together aerospace innovators and putting innovation in the spotlight.

Its accelerator program was launched to help startups grow from pre-seed to Series A. Whereas many traditional tech incubators run programs to guide companies at pre-seed ideation, Starburst offers thirteen-week cohort programs as well as twelve months of commercialization with post-seed companies to help scale and connect with leading aerospace-industry champions. Participants, who typically already have capital, receive guidance on mass manufacturing, attaining certification standards for flight, and operating their product within the aerospace industry's complex regulatory environment. The accelerator works with both aerospace technology companies pursuing other markets (such as drone tech in telecommunications) and enabling-technology companies looking to break into the aerospace supply chain (for example, in blockchain, sensors, robotics or artificial intelligence).

Though Starburst operates in multiple cities, LA is an essential location to its mission, as the city has historically been home to power players in the aerospace industry. Since the local startup community's explosion over recent years, there have been two powerful scenes for innovation: heritage aerospace companies and startups developing new products. The accelerator bridges the gap between the two, forging collaboration for mutual innovation. This year, Starburst announced a new program: its first joint Techstars Starburst Space Accelerator. Backed by NASA's Jet Propulsion Laboratory, the U.S. Air Force, Lockheed Martin, SAIC, Maxar Technologies and IAI North America, it will nurture earlier-stage companies in Los Angeles in the space and frontier technology sphere.

[Apply to]
f6s.com/starburst

[Links]
Web: **starburst.aero** Twitter: **@starburstinnov** Instagram: **starburstaero**

- **Start with a strong team.**
  Because we invest so early and see so many companies, we are very focused on the founding team. That's a lot more important than what the idea is or whether the company has raised money previously.

- **Have the right qualities.**
  We look for curiosity, passion, intellectual honesty, grit, resilience and a sense of humor.

- **Think long term.**
  We want to know that the team can make it for the long haul.

- **Fit the investment criteria.**
  In terms of investment areas, we invest across the spectrum of tech-enabled businesses: retail, ecommerce and supply chain, enterprise SAAS, media and entertainment, mobility and logistics, digital health, fintech and even CPG.

[Name]
Techstars LA

[Elevator Pitch]
"We are the global network that helps entrepreneurs succeed. We offer a wealth of opportunities for entrepreneurs, anchored by our mentorship-driven accelerator programs through which we invest in, mentor and support top early-stage companies around the world."

[Sector]
Multiple

[Description]
Techstars LA, now in its third year, is both a network for budding entrepreneurs and a program that focuses on accelerating early-stage startups over an intensive three-month program. Techstars is truly a global company. It got its start in Boulder, Colorado, in 2007 and now operates in 168 countries, with a portfolio of two thousand startups serving a community of over ten thousand alumni and mentors. It now operates three programs in LA: its main City program, which is aimed at incubating local startups, and two others focused on space and music. The yearly Techstars LA program lasts for twelve weeks and matches ten early-stage companies with mentors who help founders determine the best ways to drive growth. In addition to mentorship, the program provides a number of other resources, including $120,000 in capital, fundraising support and business development assistance. "Our program is not 'startup school,'" says Anna Barber, managing director of Techstars LA. "There's not a lot in Techstars that feels like classroom content. It's about the process of building a company, and we provide a laboratory to do that in that's incredibly effective."

LA-based companies to go through the Techstars LA program have spanned the gamut of industries and markets, everything from Fernish, a furniture subscription company, to Slingshot Aerospace, a satellite-data platform. Companies come into the program with different needs, which the program's mentors help identify alongside the founders. "Some want to find product-market fit, others want to prove revenue or successfully launch their product, others have fundraising goals," Anna says. "Our job is to help founders figure out what that next goal should be and then achieve it."

[Apply to]
techstars.com/apply

[Links]
Web: **techstars.com** Facebook: **techstars** Twitter: **@techstars** Instagram: **techstars**

- **Deliver a solution to a problem in a scalable way.**
  We look for businesses that will thrive in the long term. What problem are you solving, and how will you deliver that solution in a scalable way?

- **Have women founders.**
  Women Founders Network aims to rectify the dearth of capital equity invested in women founders. We partner with businesses specifically founded by women to help them work toward professional capital investment.

- **Be at the seed stage.**
  To best benefit from our program, companies need to be past the idea stage. We work with seed-stage companies with an existing proof of concept.

- **Have no investor capital.**
  We help enterprises move toward the milestone of initial professional capital investment. Therefore, we work only with companies that have not yet received this type of funding.

Women Founders Network

[Name]

[Elevator Pitch] *"We operate as a venture catalyst. We try to get women that have scalable, investible businesses initial help, mentorship, sponsorship and support so they can eventually get professional capital invested in their company."*

[Sector] **Women-founded companies across verticals**

[Description] Women Founders Network works to increase venture capital invested in women-founded companies. The project grew out of a networking group among women executives who sought to counteract gender discrimination in the business world by providing support and opportunities to one another. With the understanding that entrepreneurship is the way to general capital equity, the network was created to mentor, support and help emerging women-run businesses work toward receiving professional capital investment. Currently, only two percent of startups with funding are run by women. The Women Founders Network strives to raise the percentage to fifty through mentorship and exposure opportunities that help women-founded companies attain the funding needed to scale their businesses.

To do this, Women Founders Network offers ongoing workshops for women entrepreneurs along with its yearly Fast Pitch competition. Fast Pitch helps businesses perfect their pitch to receive funding from angel and venture capitalist investors. All applicants are eligible to attend a day of workshops supported by UCLA (University of California, Los Angeles) and held at the university. Participants receive guidance on modeling financials, constructing business plans and other issues to consider for capital raising. Through the application vetting process, the program selects ten finalists. All finalist companies receive personalized mentorship opportunities: they work with a pitch coach to help finalize and perfect their pitches, and with a financial coach to assist with business strategy. If a company needs coaching in an area specific to its mission, such as ecommerce, the program also strives to connect founders with helpful advisers. The competition distributes $150,000 worth of professional services to finalists during the preparation stage, and $50,000 in prize money to the top three companies. Regardless of a company's final placement in the competition, all ten finalists make valuable connections with the mentors and competition judges who work as leaders in the industry.

[Apply to] womenfoundersnetwork.com

[Links] Web: womenfoundersnetwork.com Facebook: womenfoundersnetwork Twitter: @womenfoundersLA

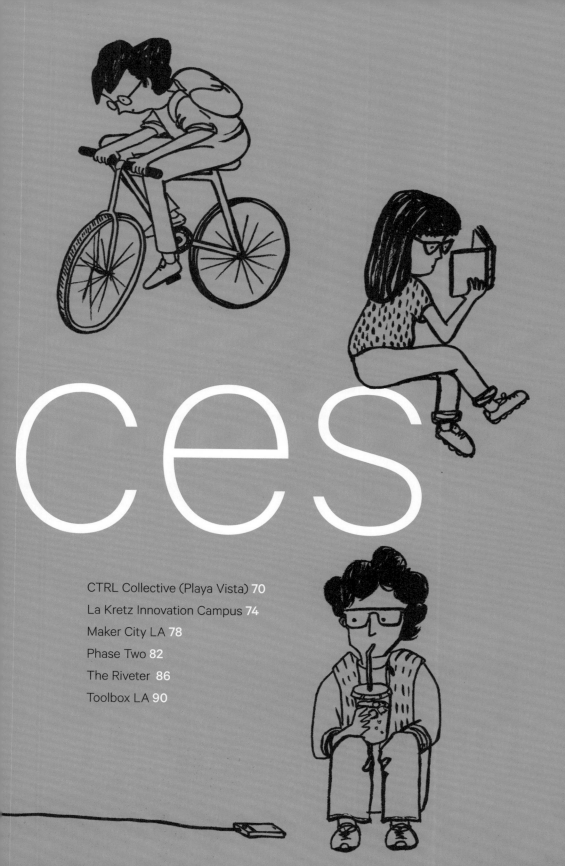

ces

[Name] # CTRL Collective (Playa Vista)

[Address] 12575 Beatrice Street, Los Angeles, CA 90066

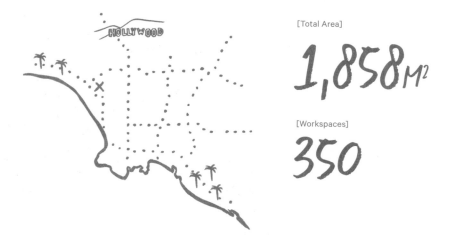

[Total Area]

1,858m²

[Workspaces]

350

[The Story] CTRL Collective aims to be the hipster coffeehouse of coworking spaces. Located in a bustling tech corridor of Los Angeles, its Playa Vista building features upscale designs, natural light and secluded, customized spaces tailored to meet the needs of facility clientele. While its members work predominantly in some form of tech, the space brings together professionals developing ventures of varying sizes from startup to established enterprise, and across diverse subsectors including software development and virtual reality.

CTRL Collective offers its members internet, open workspaces, private phone booths, meeting rooms and creation labs. They also receive 24/7 building access, access to mail and printing services, and available snacks. A converted garage on the property includes a makerspace and art studio. Member-appreciation weeks encourage engagement and intercompany pollination, and a current priority is investing further into the community and bringing CTRL Collective workers together. Most new clients come in through referrals from existing members. In addition to its Playa Vista location, CTRL Collective has spaces in Pasadena, Manhattan Beach and Denver.

[Links] Web: **ctrlcollective.com** Facebook: **ctrlcollective** Twitter: **@ctrlcollective** Instagram: **ctrlcollective**

Face of the Space:
Avi Zolty is the chief marketing officer at CTRL Collective. One of the first patrons to walk into the original CTRL Collective building in Playa Vista, he now oversees operations with a focus on member engagement, marketing infrastructure and refining services to best meet client needs.

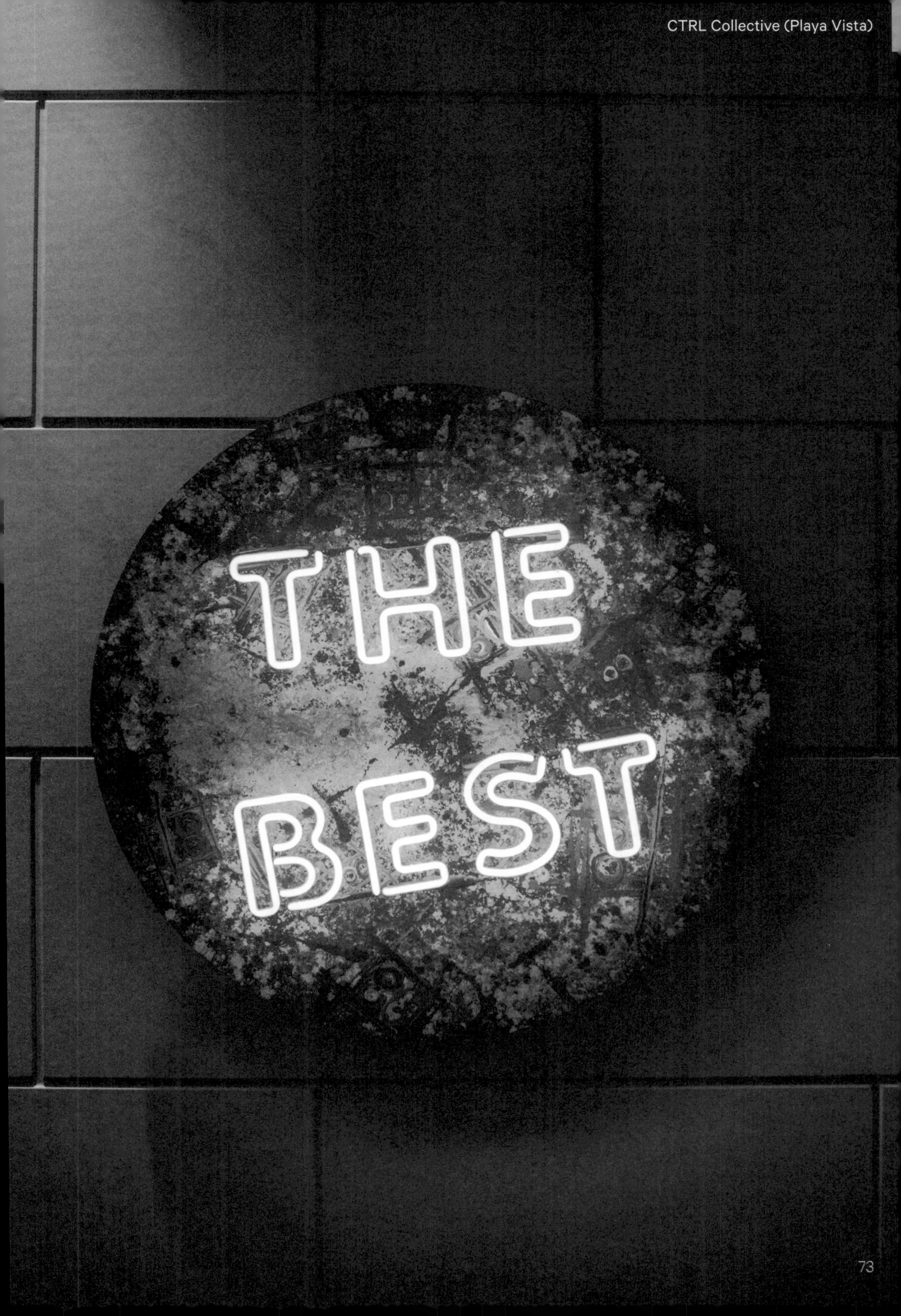
THE
BEST

La Kretz Innovation Campus

[Name]

[Address]   525 S Hewitt Street, Los Angeles, CA 90013

[Total Area]

12,950 M²

[Desks]

235

[The Story]   With over two dozen active portfolio companies, LACI is creating an inclusive green economy. The La Kretz Innovation Campus – a former furniture manufacturing plant that was completely retrofitted into a coworking space – is publicly owned by the LADWP (Los Angeles Department of Water and Power). As steward of this impressive facility, LACI was able to tailor the space to fit the needs of contemporary cleantech startups. It provides coworking memberships to 115 community organizations and offers a light-soaked, conversation-conducive open-plan space. Features include a dedicated coworking section and the region's most advanced prototyping center, which includes 3D printers and a wet lab, electronics lab and welding shop. The 3.2-acre (12,950 m2) campus was designed by John Friedman Alice Kimm Architects and utilizes green technology, including a solar canopy and bioswales.

The La Kretz Campus is approved for LEED Platinum rating and houses LA's first public greywater filtration and microgrid systems. With thousands of visitors each year, the campus serves as a platform to educate and inspire with student field trips, STEAM programming and workforce development, offering opportunity and accessibility to the green economy to communities all over LA.

Face of the Space:

Matt Petersen is the president and CEO of the Los Angeles Cleantech Incubator (LACI). In his former position as the chief sustainability officer for the City of Los Angeles, he acted as the chief architect of the Sustainable City pLAn. Matt cofounded Global Green USA, is chair of the Climate Mayors board and is a board member of Habitat for Humanity of Greater LA, the Center for Environmental Health, and the Sir Edmund Hillary Institute for International Leadership.

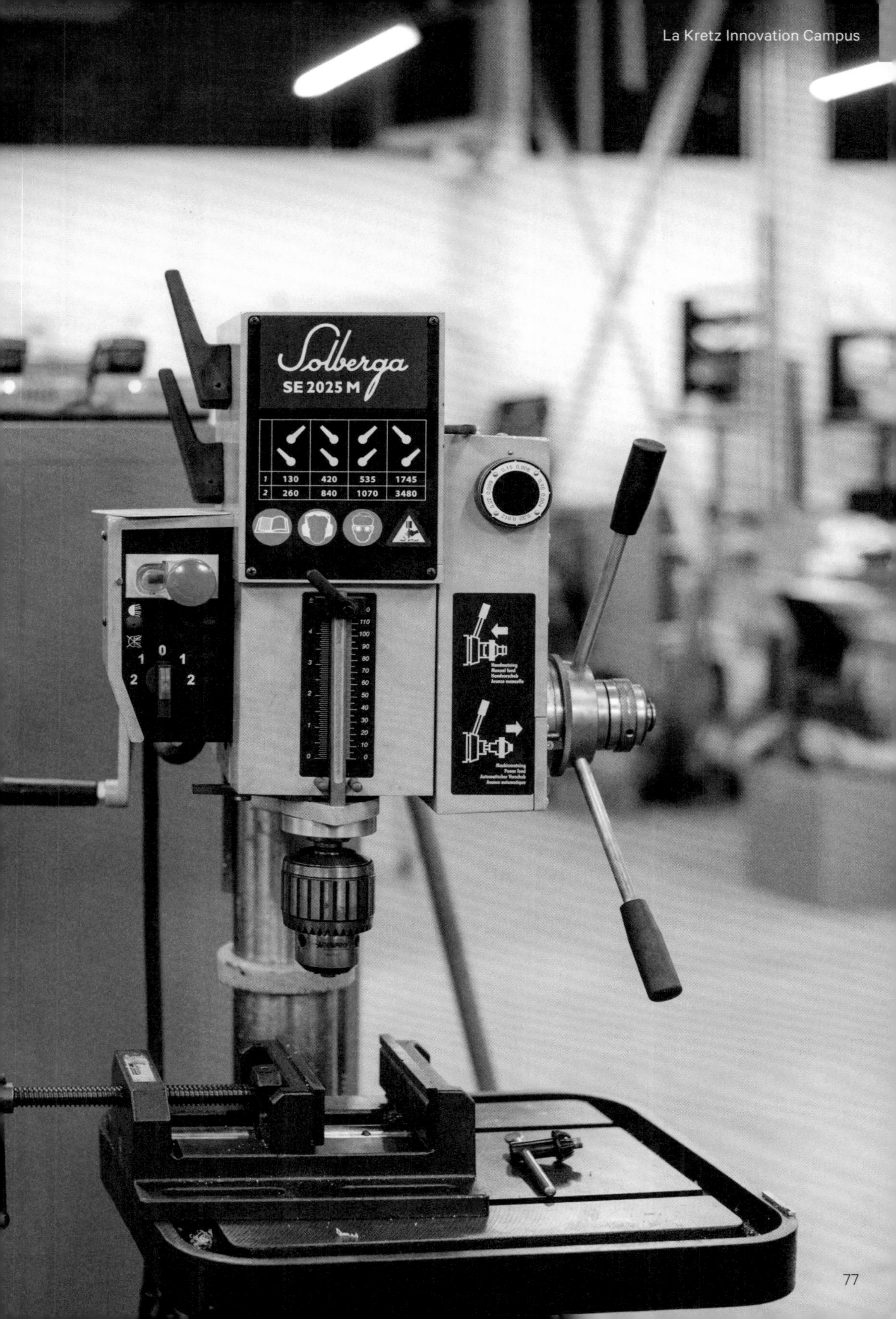
Solberga
SE 2025 M
1 130 420 535 1745
2 260 840 1070 3480

[Name] # Maker City LA

[Address] 1933 S. Broadway, Los Angeles, CA 90007

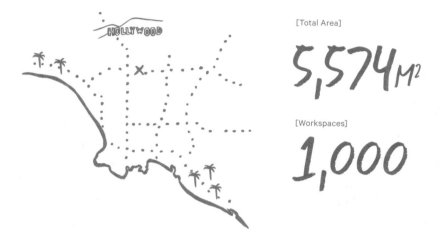

[Total Area]

5,574m²

[Workspaces]

1,000

[The Story] Maker City LA launched in 2013 as a workspace for the creative businesses, entrepreneurs and makers of the entertainment-production and apparel industries. Now its members also include nonprofits, licensed practitioners and startups. Maker City LA offers traditional coworking desks and small and large offices for short- or long-term leasing. Production rooms, such as a podcast studio, a spray booth, and film and photo studios, are also available to rent, in addition to meeting spaces, conference rooms and event spaces.

The coworking space is located on the eleventh floor of The Reef, a multipurpose "creative habitat" workspace. Three distinct entities conjoin within the building to address myriad creative needs: Maker City LA; LA Mart, which houses showrooms for home and lifestyle lines; and Magic Box, which rivals the Long Beach Convention Center as a venue for events and trade shows. The perks of working in the building include discounts to the media lab and the use of a green screen. Diverse creatives can forge connections over lunch in the building's cafe, at the weekly food trucks, or at Maker City LA's regular community breakfast. Located in the emerging artistic and tech hub of Downtown LA, The Reef values its community feel, where, for example, a tech entrepreneur dealing with a parking ticket can pop in for assistance at the law office of Roberts and Roberts and speak with a friendly attorney.

[Links] Web: **MakerCityLA.com** Facebook: **MakerCityLA** Twitter: **@MakerCityLA** Instagram: **MakerCityLA**

Face of the Space:

Teresa Garcia is the general manager at Maker City LA. She joined the team back in 2013 when Maker City LA was just 5,574 m² of empty space. She focuses on business development and on crafting practical strategies to execute the company's overall mission statement and its work toward viability.

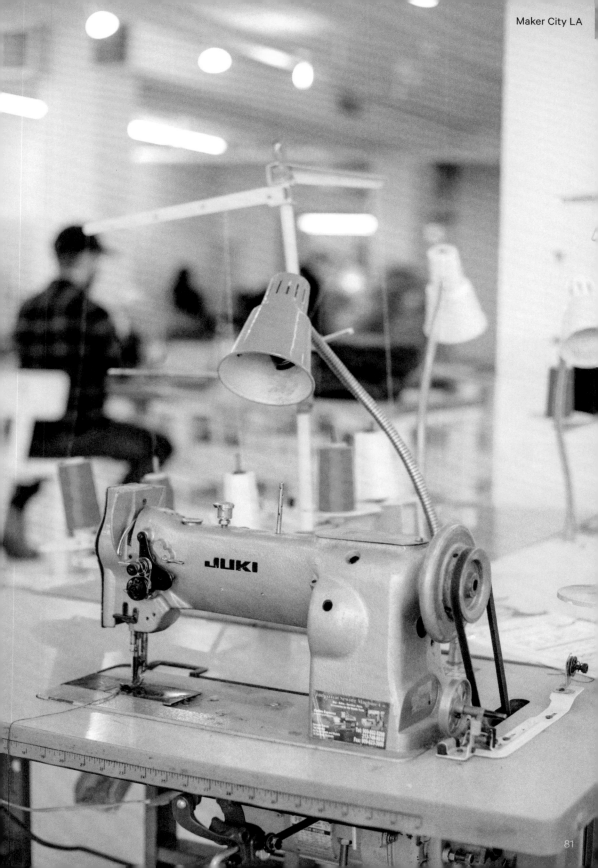

[Name]

Phase Two

[Address]   5877 Obama Boulevard, Los Angeles, California 90016

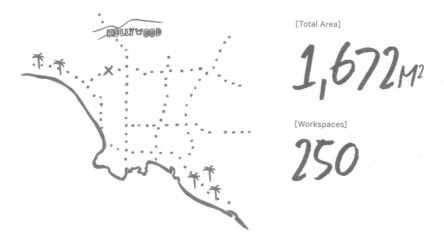

[Total Area]

1,672M²

[Workspaces]

250

[The Story]   Founded in late 2017, the aptly named Phase Two offers innovators in the tech, media and entertainment industries a home base to develop their projects after their initial launch process. Creators who've moved out of the garage phase can intermingle and learn from one another under one roof in a space that offers a green-screen room, free internet, a library, meeting areas, coworking spaces, private phone booths, mail and printing services and housekeeping. With 24/7 access to the sleekly designed building, members can leave behind stuffy office environments to work at long kitchen tables, cozy couch nooks or on the front or back patio. They can also take advantage of available virtual reality panels, host gatherings in event spaces and even bring their dogs to work.

By catering to more than one specific industry, Phase Two offers a chance for even small teams to join a bustling and diverse community. Programmers mingle with journalists and artists, expanding their knowledge across fields through conversations over free coffee, beer or wine in curated communal areas.

[Links]   Web: **phasetwospace.com** Facebook: **phasetwospace** Twitter: **@phasetwospace**

Face of the Space:
Dan Pastewka is the manager of Phase Two and one of the initial cofounders. He first got the idea to launch Phase Two with his business partner after exposure to accelerators in the Los Angeles and Bay Areas, seeing the opportunity to bring entrepreneurs together in the still-emerging startup scene of Los Angeles. He spent two years scouring city real estate to find the perfect space before moving into operations.

[Name]
The Riveter

[Address]   4505 Glencoe Ave. Marina Del Rey, CA 90292

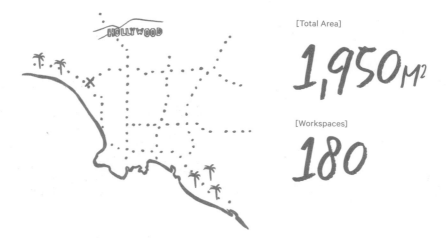

[Total Area]

1,950M²

[Workspaces]

180

[The Story]   The Riveter, which describes itself as "built by women, for everyone," originated in Seattle as the brainchild of entrepreneur Amy Nelson. The space was founded with the vision of creating "a world in which equity of opportunity in work and business is not a promise, but is a reality," says Miesha Baker, senior manager of Public Relations and Communications at the Riveter.

It may have grown up in the Pacific Northwest, but it found its second home in California when it expanded to Los Angeles in June of 2018. The aim was to bring more inclusivity to the LA tech world through providing flexible membership options and a revolving door of visiting tech leaders, venture capitalists and others. The Riveter is right at home with the airy vibes of the Californian coast and has two LA locations: one in West LA and their second location in Marina Del Rey. The Marina Del Rey space moves away from the rustic-cabin aesthetics of Seattle in favor of high ceilings, white tabletops and an industrial chic layout. It offers amenities like a greenroom, podcast room, a commercial printer and a mothers' room.

[Links]   Web: **theriveter.co** Facebook: **theriverterco** Twitter: **@theriveterco** Instagram: **theriverterco**

Face of the Space:

Heather Carter is the national managing director at the Riveter. She has nearly a decade of founder and executive-level experience in operations and business development, having scaled companies in consumer tech and recurring revenue models, both geographically and vertically from pre-seed to series C. Heather was the founding operator of Soothe, massages on demand; Director of Operations at Heal, doctors to your door; and COO of Helpr, an employer-sponsored childcare company.

[Name] # Toolbox LA

[Address] 9410 Owensmouth Avenue, Chatsworth, CA 91311

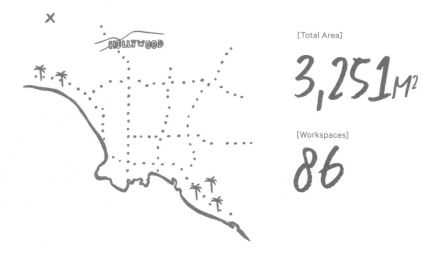

[Total Area]

3,251M²

[Workspaces]

86

[The Story] Located in the San Fernando Valley, Toolbox LA was conceived as a way to help put Southern California on the map as a hub for hardware tech. The space is also home to a biotech lab, a makerspace to help founders bring prototypes to life, and MiLA (Make in LA), an application-based hardware accelerator program. At Toolbox LA, entrepreneurs building companies from the ground up will find access to both machinery and business resources such as office hours to work toward launch and subsequent developmental milestones.

While Los Angeles is replete with coworking spaces geared toward software companies, Toolbox LA aims to foster community among creators across diverse creative and entrepreneurial industries, with particular focus on those working in hardware and looking for a hub north of the center of LA. Budding biotech founders can take advantage of wet-lab and 3D-printing services, while creatives are drawn to artist studios and a gallery showcasing member work. Coworking residents have access to lockers, meeting rooms, internet and a multifaceted event space. Cold brew and kombucha flow freely on tap.

[Links] Web: **toolbox.la** Facebook: **toolboxla** Twitter: **@ToolboxLA** Instagram: **toolboxLA**

Face of the Space:

Eager to join the budding Los Angeles startup scene, Carmen Palafox teamed up with her Toolbox LA partners after completing an executive MBA program at UC Berkeley. She manages overall company operations with a particular focus on the MiLA venture capital fund, helping companies to develop financial strategies to scale with additional capital.

erts

Yvette Bellamy and Hicham Mhanna / BCG Digital Ventures

People & Operations Director, North America
VP Engineering

[Sector]   **Digital Innovation**

Launching a startup from scratch is never easy, but the journey can be incredibly rewarding. Yvette Bellamy, the People and Operations Director in North America at BCG Digital Ventures (overseeing offices across Los Angeles, New York, Silicon Valley and Seattle) and Hicham Mhanna, the VP of Engineering, shared some essentials with us on building up a business from the ground up.

First, they believe that staying lean in the early days – in the operational sense and in terms of not building more than you need – is important to keep in mind. Conserve your resources and focus on finding a product-market fit. "You can outsource almost anything operational until you're ready to scale, and it's okay to not have all that figured out in the beginning," says Yvette. "Don't be afraid to reach out to experts to ensure you're on point but remember not to overengineer your operations."

Founded in 2014, BCG Digital Ventures builds and invests in startups alongside its corporate partners. Ventures in their portfolio include Regi (a booking platform for medical aesthetic and beauty treatments, built alongside pharmaceutical company Allergan) and HeyCar (an online platform for used cars, launched in partnership with Volkswagen Financial Services in Germany). Bringing startups and corporates together in their ventures means both parties can learn from each other during the process. Most of BCG Digital Ventures' team members, who are spread across its seven centers in Manhattan Beach, Berlin, London, New York, Sydney, Shanghai and Tokyo, consist of former startup founders and employees.

"Our methodology takes the mindset of a startup and applies it to the assets of a corporate, meaning a corporate has an accessible way to practice innovation and the startup has a higher chance of success," says Hicham. For instance, startups can learn about being proactive in thinking about risks and good scenario planning, while corporates can learn about allowing ideas and innovation to thrive without working in silos and ensuring they have permission to fail.

Most important tips for startups:

- **Keep your startup lean at the beginning of your journey.**
  Conserve your resources. The early days should be about
  finding a product-market fit and validating your idea. Don't
  spend your hard-earned or hard-raised money building
  something you don't need.

- **Remember that technology isn't just a means to an end.**
  Don't build technology just to build it; tech should serve
  a bigger goal and solve a problem in a sector or industry.

- **Surround yourself with a great team of people.** Hire a
  dream team of people who believe in the product or service
  you're offering and complement each other with their skills.

For fledgling entrepreneurs trying to get their business off the ground, Hicham advises them not to think about technology as a means to an end. "The goal isn't to build technology just to build it," he says. "Remember that tech serves a much bigger role, like solving major pain points in sectors such as healthcare or logistics, to name a few." In addition to working with and supporting the firm's engineering teams to build innovative products for corporate partners, Hicham is a general manager (GM) for one of BCG Digital Ventures' startups in the AI and machine-learning space. He explains that being a GM for a venture or startup means taking the responsibility of executing a strategy from beginning to end.

A startup is nothing without the people behind it. That's why hiring a passionate and talented team is critical to the success of your business. "You don't need a cofounder for the sake of it," says Yvette, who works on understanding what people and operations infrastructures are needed at BCG Digital Ventures in order to continue to scale the business. "You can back yourself up by having a great team of people around you, but don't forget to give yourself the flexibility to change the team up if you need to as your business scales."

In Los Angeles, BCG Digital Ventures is very active in the startup community. The team hosts a number of meetups and hackathons for entrepreneurs, many of which provide a platform for innovators to demo their technology. "The unique startups we create here have a higher likelihood of success than the average startup," says Hicham. "We build these companies with influential businesses from around the world that can bring resources, brand equity, an existing customer base and other assets to the table."

About

BCG Digital Ventures is a corporate investment and incubation firm. It invents, builds, scales and invests in startups with the world's most influential companies. BCG Digital Ventures shares risk and invests alongside its corporate and startup partners via a range of collaborative options. Founded in 2014, it has seven major innovation and investment centers (in Manhattan Beach, Berlin, London, New York, Sydney, Shanghai and Tokyo) and several Labs, or satellite locations, including Silicon Valley and Seattle, with more locations opening soon.

[Contact]   Email: yvette.bellamy@bcgdv.com / hicham.mhanna@bcgdv.com

[Links]   Web: bcgdv.com Facebook: BCGDV Twitter: @bcgdv Instagram: bcgdv

" *You can outsource almost anything operational until you're ready to scale, and it's okay to not have all that figured out in the beginning.* "

Patrick Anding and Richard Friedman / DLA Piper LLP (US)

Partner
Of Counsel

[Sector]   **Legal**

For many people, Los Angeles is associated with glitz, glam and great weather. However, more and more, the city is becoming known for its growing startup ecosystem.

"There was a time when LA was not known as a tech epicenter, but that has changed," says Patrick Anding, a partner in DLA Piper's Emerging Growth and Venture Capital practice in LA. "Entrepreneurs from all over the world are coming here to start businesses and take advantage of the ecosystem that has developed here, including the substantial influx of venture capital funds available in the LA market. There's a fantastic talent pool, real estate is relatively affordable compared to Silicon Valley, and the community is inclusive and supportive."

Richard Friedman, of counsel in DLA Piper's Emerging Growth and Venture Capital practice in LA, agrees and adds that LA's market is becoming much more diversified. "There was a time when LA was known mostly for consumer, lifestyle, media and advertising startups," he says, "but now we're seeing significant activity across a range of industries, such as clean energy, space, fintech and medical- and health-related technologies. This growth can be attributed in part to the top-tier universities and wealth of technical talent and creative talent our city is blessed with."

With lawyers located in more than forty countries around the world, DLA Piper is a global business law firm with clients ranging from multinational, Global 1000 and Fortune 500 enterprises to burgeoning startups developing innovative technologies. Both Patrick and Rick advise startups and emerging companies from company formation and initial financing to an exit event.

"In addition to having offices worldwide, what sets DLA Piper apart is that we have deep experience outside of the traditional high-growth tech industry," says Patrick. "We offer a full suite of business legal resources to help companies operating in the hospitality, gaming, entertainment and real estate industries and practically every other sector."

Most important tips for startups:

- Seek legal counsel early on to avoid expensive pitfalls. This is particularly important when you begin to sell products or services, or when multiple stakeholders begin to have an interest in your startup. In both cases, it's crucial that you have set up your business properly and maintained the appropriate documentation for these relationships.

- Have an intellectual-property strategy in place from day one. Ensure you have the correct IP agreements in place with all founders as well as other service providers and partners.

- Be involved in the legal process and ask questions. While it's important to find a lawyer that understands your business and its trajectory, it's recommended that founders have an open and ready-to-learn mindset when approaching legal decisions.

Patrick and Rick shared insights on how startups can set themselves up for success from a legal perspective and what founders can do to increase their chances of attracting investors, bringing products or services to market and building valuable businesses. They say that for founders, a key step to avoid expensive pitfalls along the way is to involve legal counsel early on, particularly when beginning to sell products or services or when multiple stakeholders begin to have an interest in the organization.

"In both cases, it's important to speak to a lawyer to ensure you have set up your business properly and have the proper documentation for these relationships," says Patrick. Since corporations typically organize relationships between their stakeholders (founders, investors, employees, creditors, taxing authorities, regulators and customers), he adds that founders need to structure the business to manage these relationships as early as they can. "Postponing that process and forging ahead without properly documenting these relationships can be costly and time-consuming to clean up later."

Additionally, two areas where founders should pay attention and seek the advice of experienced counsel are the company cap table and intellectual property (IP). "There are a lot of potential cap-table pitfalls, like issuing equity without vesting, committing equity informally through emails or texts, committing to issue a certain percentage of the company, failing to make the necessary tax election for unvested founder shares, failing to understand the economics of convertibles notes or safes, or simply issuing more equity than is warranted for a particular role," says Richard. "IP protection also needs to be considered from day one, including developing an IP strategy to create a competitive advantage, ensuring proper IP agreements are in place with all founders, other service providers and partners, and making sure founders aren't using IP owned by former employers."

When looking for legal counsel, it's crucial to find a lawyer who understands your business and its trajectory. This knowledge, coupled with industry insight, will influence the quality of counsel you receive. Moreover, it helps to have an open and ready-to-learn mindset, not only when running your startup but also when approaching legal decisions. "Find lawyers you trust, and get engaged with the process," says Patrick. "It's your business. Own it and be proactive."

About
DLA Piper is a global law firm with lawyers located in more than forty countries throughout the Americas, Europe, the Middle East, Africa and Asia Pacific, positioning it to help clients with their legal needs around the world. The firm offers practical and innovative legal solutions that help its clients succeed.

[Contact] Email: **patrick.anding@dlapiper.com / richard.friedman@dlapiper.com**
Telephone: **+1 310 595 3000**

[Links] Web: **dlapiper.com/en/us** Facebook: **DLAPiperGlobal** Twitter: **@DLA_Piper**

"Find lawyers you trust, and get engaged with the process."

Kory Chapelle and Gustavo Esquivel / Early Growth Financial Services

LA Market Managers

[Sector]   **Financial Services**

Being a founder at a startup means that, at any point in time, you may be juggling a bunch of tasks ranging from sales and marketing to operations and fundraising. So it's easy to put your finances on hold when trying to get your business off the ground, especially if it's not your area of expertise. However, Kory Chapelle and Gustavo Esquivel, LA Market Managers at Early Growth Financial Services (EGFS), believe that it's essential for startups to prioritize accounting, taxes and finances sooner rather than later.

Founded in 2008, EGFS is a financial services firm that works with startups across the US, with operations in Los Angeles, Silicon Valley, San Francisco, Chicago, Seattle, Portland and New York City. The company acts as a one-stop shop for founders, offering support in these main areas: startup tax and compliance, accounting services, business valuations (such as 409A valuations), fund accounting and administration, and CFO consulting.

For those who aren't familiar with the concept of outsourced CFO consulting, Kory says EGFS maintains a stable of chief finance officers who provide strategic guidance to startups in a variety of ways. CFOs can help with everything from budgeting and forecasting to financial modeling, revenue recognition, fundraising and more. "We strategically align CFOs with companies where they can provide the most value, depending on their vertical, stage and business model," he says. "Ultimately, it's about mitigating issues before they happen and thinking long term about your finances."

In addition to financial services, the EGFS team is very active in the startup ecosystem. They host several events, provide mentorship at accelerators and incubators, hold webinars and offer valuable resources on their blog (**earlygrowthfinancialservices.com/blog**). Startups working with EGFS get the opportunity to tap into an extensive network of players in the startup scene, including VCs, marketing agencies, HR/payroll firms, banks and law firms. "We're here to help startups be more efficient with their time, connect them with the right people and increase their chances for success," says Gustavo.

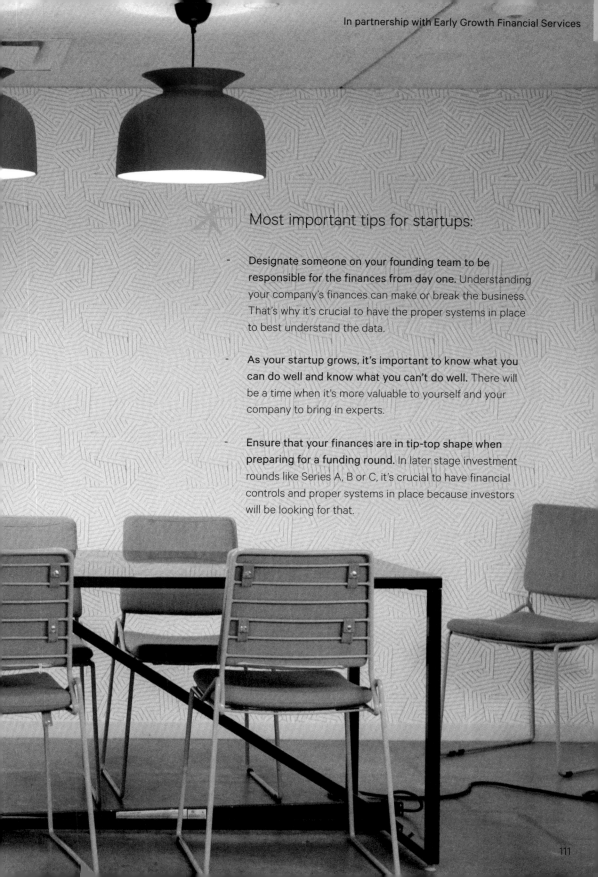

Most important tips for startups:

- **Designate someone on your founding team to be responsible for the finances from day one.** Understanding your company's finances can make or break the business. That's why it's crucial to have the proper systems in place to best understand the data.

- **As your startup grows, it's important to know what you can do well and know what you can't do well.** There will be a time when it's more valuable to yourself and your company to bring in experts.

- **Ensure that your finances are in tip-top shape when preparing for a funding round.** In later stage investment rounds like Series A, B or C, it's crucial to have financial controls and proper systems in place because investors will be looking for that.

A company's finances can make or break its business. That's why it's crucial to have a good grasp of what's going on with your startup's finances from day one. "If you have two or more cofounders, it's important to have a conversation about who will be in charge of keeping track of everything," explains Gustavo. At least one person in the company needs to take responsibility for this part of the business. Otherwise, there's a risk that your numbers will be in disarray, which can lead to misinformed decisions or leaving a bad impression on potential investors.

There's no doubt that, early on, founders are wearing many hats and doing the finance themselves; however, Kory stresses that it's essential as a founder to know your limitations. Know what you can do well, and know what you can't do well. "There comes a time when it's more valuable to bring in experts," he says. "This allows entrepreneurs to spend more time and energy focusing on the company and its customers."

As a startup grows, it's only natural that the systems and tools used to manage its finances evolve with it. It makes sense to use cost-effective tools in the early stages. As any successful entrepreneur can tell you, success depends on more than merely having a good product/service offering. The business issues are what will make or break you. "EGFS has expertise in providing just-in-time financial support for small businesses, from fundraising to cash management to strategic planning to financial projections to creating and implementing simple financial systems that work," says Kory.

To stay updated on future EFGS events and to be invited to webinars, Kory and Gustavo highly recommend signing up for the newsletter on their website.

About
EGFS is the nation's largest outsource/fractional accounting firm in the startup space. It is headquartered in Silicon Valley with offices in SF, LA, NY, Seattle, Portland, Chicago, Boston and more. EGFS has four pillars of service: corporate taxes, valuation services (specializing in the 409A), accounting and CFO services. With relationships deep in the startup ecosystem, EGFS can add additional value by making introductions and opening doors to banks, law firms, HR, marketing and investors.

"*There comes a time when it's more valuable to bring in experts. This allows entrepreneurs to spend more time and energy focusing on the company and its customers.*"

Ann Rosenberg
/ SAP Next-Gen

Senior Vice President for UN Partnerships at SAP & Global Head
of SAP Next-Gen

[Sector]   **Innovation with purpose**

With technology advancing at unprecedented speeds, many major cities are transforming into
entrepreneurship and innovation hubs, each with a distinct identity linked to its culture and
history. Los Angeles, a gravitational center of arts and media, is now entering the world stage
as a technology hub and, according to senior vice president and global head of SAP Next-
Gen Ann Rosenberg, it's poised to become an innovation center founded on and inspired by
science-fiction thinking and Innovation 4.0.

"I predict LA will be the next big, global innovation hub, based on the concentration of science-
fiction knowledge in the region and its position as the center of the US entertainment industry,"
says Ann. Originally from Denmark and now based in New York City, Ann is an international
advocate for purpose-driven innovation. She educates startups and corporates on the concept
of Innovation 4.0, which aligns science-fiction thinking and purpose-driven thinking with the
UN's seventeen Sustainable Development Goals (SDGs or Global Goals) to unlock profit and
social-purpose potential for exponential technologies.

The SDGs, established in 2015 by world leaders from UN member states, aim to create a better
future by 2030; namely, by confronting issues such as hunger and poverty and ensuring
gender equality and good-quality healthcare and education for everyone. Ann and her team
work to support and inspire the next generation of entrepreneurs and innovators in developing
impactful solutions to present and future problems, and science-fiction thinking is a vital
ingredient in this process.

In support of her vision, Ann's book on science-fiction thinking and Innovation 4.0, entitled
Science Fiction – A Starship for Enterprise Innovation, uses science-fiction tropes such as time
travel to inspire innovators to leverage their farthest-reaching imaginations in developing their
business ideas. Ann says, "We inspire purpose-driven innovators to picture themselves in the
year 2030 and imagine that the Sustainable Development Goals have been achieved, and to
focus on the opportunities for achieving positive outcomes rather than being limited
by perceptions of what is possible today."

Most important tips for startups:

- **Realize the opportunity of Los Angeles as a science-fiction city.** When you take on the task of being a big innovation hub, you should own that identity and what it stands for. Los Angeles is a new home for the science-fiction mindset and Innovation 4.0, and supporting that identity will make you better and more purpose-driven innovators.

- **Unlock your science-fiction thinking and imaginations.** Make sure you use the science-fiction mindset in building your startup, thereby aligning with the idea of Los Angeles as a science-fiction city. Your idea should be bold and futuristic to reflect the swift pace of innovation.

- **Begin to use a new value system of winning.** In your startup, start redefining success. Winning is not just about money or notoriety; it's about having a lasting impact on the future and working toward the SDGs.

<EXIT

For Ann and SAP Next-Gen, science-fiction thinking is essential for innovation, and it gives startups a competitive advantage as intelligent enterprises seek out innovation with purpose. Unlocking creativity through science-fiction thinking can help companies adopt an innovation mindset to deal with unprecedented surges in technological advancement and transform it into disruptive, purpose-driven innovation.

Ann believes that Los Angeles is an ideal innovation city to take on the mantle of a science-fiction hub. The magnitude of creativity in the city can act as inspiration for startups to unlock the potential of technologies in reaching the SDGs. "When you want to make some really big changes, you need a bold mindset," says Ann. "LA has the right ingredients to foster that mindset and is an outstanding setting for science fiction-inspired innovation with purpose."

However, adopting science-fiction thinking is not the end of the story; in her book and at speaking engagements, Ann urges startups and corporates to redefine not only what they're doing but also where they want to go. "With the science-fiction mindset, companies will accelerate toward good ideas," says Ann, "so how are we going to measure whether they lead toward a winning strategy?"

Science-fiction thinking can help entrepreneurs redefine winning so that it's about contributing to the next generation of innovators and innovating more sustainably. "If you look today at some of the most successful people in the world, it's not about money; it's about the impact they are driving as human beings." If Los Angeles is able to own its identity as a science-fiction innovation center, startups and corporates founding in the region and those migrating there can work together and innovate toward the most meaningful impact.

SAP Next-Gen is leading initiatives and creating spaces to help accelerate LA as an innovation hub on the world stage and take full advantage of the science-fiction imagination already so prevalent in the city. To drive Los Angeles to meet this innovative future, SAP Next-Gen is collaborating with a number of notable universities, such as the University of Southern California, and is opening a concept office with coworking space called Hanahaus at Newport Beach. SAP's Innovation Center Network also opened a residency at the Cove at UCI Applied Innovation.

About

SAP Next-Gen is a purpose-driven innovation university and community linked to the UN Global Goals and supporting SAP's customers across 25 industries in over 180 countries. The community leverages 3,700+ educational institutions in 116 countries, 150+ SAP Next-Gen labs/hubs at universities, partner and SAP locations, 160+ SAP Next-Gen Chapters, 25+ innovation communities through a partnership with Startup Guide, and a growing global network of 30+ FQ Lounges @ Campus, as well as startups, accelerators, tech community partners, venture firms, futurists and purpose-driven institutions.

[Contact]   Email: **ann.rosenberg@sap.com**

[Links]   Web: **sap.com/next-gen** Facebook: **SAPNextGen** Twitter: **@SAPNextGen**

"If you look today at some of the most successful people in the world, it's not about money; it's about the impact they are driving as human beings."

ders

Brent Bushnell

CEO and Cofounder / Two Bit Circus

Brent Bushnell is the CEO of Two Bit Circus, an experiential entertainment company whose micro-amusement park in downtown Los Angeles features virtual reality games, escape rooms and modernized adventure experiences geared toward a tech-savvy generation. He's board president of the nonprofit Two Bit Circus Foundation, which uses play to inspire youth about STEM disciplines. He's also an Edmund Hillary Fellow and a UCLA-trained engineer and was previously the on-camera inventor for ABC's Extreme Makeover: Home Edition. He supports Clowns Without Borders and serves as a mentor for teen entrepreneurs.

Tell me about the genesis of Two Bit Circus. Where did the idea come from and what need were you trying to fill?
At first it was really just my cofounder and I having fun making interactive art we could take to parties. Our main thesis even in 2008 was that everybody's on their phones and on Facebook, but we're social animals: getting together live is the best. We wanted lots of new ways to get people playing together, particularly at events. The simplest thing can be the best icebreaker. So we were smashing together whatever technology we could find into attractions that we could bring to events. Those events got bigger and bigger. All of a sudden were doing all the entertainment for Amazon's holiday party and that kind of stuff.

What was your background before moving into work on Two Bit Circus?
I'm trained in computer science and electrical engineering, but I've been an entrepreneur my whole life. At the time, I was running a company making web-based applications for inventory control and helping insurance and auto salvage manage their inventory. It was my own company, and that was great, but it wasn't nearly as exciting. In 2008, with the recession, I wasn't really loving what I was working on. That was when I met my cofounder. He was working at a think tank in Glendale. All their customers were basically the military. We both were looking for something else to do.

When you were first bringing your creations to parties, did you have an idea of the company you'd eventually grow into?
We loved it, so we kept experimenting with new stuff, but we didn't imagine that dragging these games around had the option to be a company. It was interesting: we built what are now called escape rooms, which didn't exist at the time. We just called them a "Live Action Adventure."

We were like, "How is this ever gonna scale? We'll just build it for our friends." It was only after brands started calling and we were doing huge events for Samsung and the Super Bowl that we started realizing, "Well, there's a consultancy here." But what's the company that can scale? We discovered the answer to that along the way, as we kept building more. We ultimately did our own traveling carnival that we toured around for two years and then finally said, "Okay, it's time to go permanent." And that led us to the park.

How did you start the transition process toward permanency?

We first did a design of all the things we wanted to put in. We did a layout. By then, we'd done public installations for eight years. We'd helped Dave and Buster's and Samsung launch their virtual reality programs. We'd made traveling escape rooms for Warner Brothers. We'd done a lot of different kinds of entertainment. But it was all more modern than traditional arcade public entertainment. What we really wanted was a home for all the stuff to live. After doing the work for all those brands, building our own stuff and doing our traveling carnival, we could see what worked in public and what didn't work. So we began by making that layout and then started fundraising for it. We partnered up with the incredible Kim Schaefer, who was the CEO of Great Wolf Lodge, a huge indoor water park and hotel chain. All of a sudden, the whole thing was real.

What were some of the early struggles you encountered? How did you overcome them?

In doing events, you learn really quickly what people like, what's complicated, and what's not complicated. People are different in public. You have to build around those differences. When you're at home, you've got time. You're comfortable, you're in your safe place. You can have a glass of wine and take your time to read the instructions. Chances are you're using something you own. But in public, you're dealing with shared things. You're maybe on a date or with a colleague. You're in a different headspace. So things had to be made with minimal instruction, be super easy and really durable. We really learned about throughput. If you have an experience that takes two hours, not a lot of people will be able to do it. If it's a virtual reality thing where you've got to put a headset on everybody, you have to optimize for that infrastructure.

In the process of building the company, what would you characterize as some of your biggest mistakes?

We went into an existing building in downtown LA that needed a ton of work. I'd probably still do it again even though we had to replace the roof and do seismic upgrade. That was terrible. For our liquor license, everybody with 10 percent ownership or more has to sign an affidavit. We have venture investors – their investors are pension bonds and what not. It was sort of impossible for those affidavits to be signed by all of their LPs. We actually won the lottery but had to give it back and sort out a new structure that was very expensive.

"Work with people you love. Find those people who are smarter than you in the domain that you want to work with them. Empower them."

What about your best decision?

The team we have has been awesome. I've loved working with Kim. She's been such a great contribution to the team. Between her and a few others, that's been fantastic.

With the wisdom of having gone through the starting up process, is there anything you wish you'd known back at the start?

Work with people you love. That old "hire slowly, fire quickly" is so true. Work with people you trust implicitly. A great entrepreneur can do lots of different things. In the beginning of your company, you wear all the hats. Ideally, when you take off the hat, you're giving it to someone doing that job better than you. Find those people who are smarter than you in the domain that you want to work with them. Empower them.

Have you found that there's a particular audience that embodies your typical customer?

We definitely have a strong millennial audience. We're great with young families and kids over seven. We also do a lot of corporate stuff, whether it's team building, events or meetings. Those three categories are, interestingly, exactly the ones we'd service when we were doing consultant work.

What about Two Bit Circus do you think taps into the millennial ethos?

I think the social element. We've seen with escape rooms and Museum of Ice Cream and immersive theater that there's a real interest and appetite for getting out in public and doing new experiences with your friends. Our games are all built around social. Most of them need three to six players to do it. So I think that's really resonated.

How have you partnered with other innovators to execute your vision for the space?

I think of this park very much like a platform. We work with lots of indie game-makers and other great creators in order to showcase their stuff. We've made a lot of the games and also worked with a lot of great creators in order to adapt their stuff for public. A game-maker makes a game for the home that's like one hundred hours of play, but in public we literally need five minutes. So adapting it is really about cutting things away in order to make it work.

What professional advice would you give founders in the early stages of starting up?
It's just critical to get going. You have an idea for whatever your project is, and it's going to change. The ideal is just, How can you get a test going this weekend? With that test, you'll learn a lot. You'll start to build an audience, and you'll be able to answer some questions. The entrepreneur is a researcher and an experimenter, and you're trying to validate your hypothesis. You want to iterate and test and be as scrappy as possible. That will give you a momentum and inform your next direction. My dad used to always say, "The entrepreneur is a doer, not a dreamer." The dream is a fine thing to do when you wake up and you're in the shower. But then you have to get going.

What do you think being based in Los Angeles adds to the space?
It's really an exciting time in LA right now. A lot of the talent that has serviced Hollywood for so long can now also serve all these other industries from video games to augmented reality and virtual reality. The Internet 1.0 and 2.0 was a lot about infrastructure and systems. Then they were sort of like, What do we do with all that stuff? 3.0 has really been about content and the kinds of things you put down those channels. And those skills are all in LA. So there's a real ecosystem now around the startup community and capital at every stage from seed to venture and private equity. We have all of the different elements that are needed to support a startup ecosystem.

[About]   Two Bit Circus is a contemporary recreation park combining classic games of yesteryear with new digital technology. Attractions include arcade and virtual reality experiences, escape rooms, live shows, and private gaming rooms.

[Links]   Web: twobitcircus.com Facebook: TwoBitCircus Twitter: @twobitcircus Instagram: twobitcircus

What are your top work essentials?
Notepad, standing desk, ergonomic keyboard.

At what age did you found your company?
Thirty.

What's your most-used app?
Pocket.

**What's the most valuable piece of advice
you've been given?**
Test immediately. If you have an idea, how can you
make a dollar this weekend?

What's your greatest skill?
Meeting with people and finding mutually beneficial
ways to collaborate.

Janice Bryant Howroyd

Founder and CEO / The ActOne Group

In 1976, Janice Bryant Howroyd left her native North Carolina with $1,500 to start a full-time employment placement business in Los Angeles. Two years later, in September 1978, she purchased a phone and a fax machine and set up shop in a former Beverly Hills rug shop. Janice, inspired in part by her experiences growing up in a big family and attending segregated schools until late high school, built ActOne Group to instill HR and strategic procurement with humanity and inclusivity. As the founder and CEO of ActOne Group, Janice is the first African American woman to own and run a billion-dollar enterprise and was even selected by former president Barack Obama as an appointee at the White House. Janice continues to have a passion for self-empowerment, mentorship and excellence in education and is active as an educator, public speaker and philanthropist.

Tell me about your entrepreneurial path. What kind of early work experiences led you to the idea of founding a company focused on workplace solutions?
Growing up in North Carolina, pre-civil rights, I did not have any particular role models for what a founder of a workforce solutions organization would look like. As a matter of fact, I wasn't even familiar with the staffing model at all. I grew up in a segregated community, and it was black and white and two Jewish families – that's it. On my side of the community, most of the people I knew who would be considered professional were teachers and preachers. Then we had day laborers. So coming into a workforce solutions environment for me was pure innovation on my part to design an organization that offers the type of service I found lacking when I looked for work years earlier when I came to Los Angeles, California.

When you did come to Los Angeles, what was your first experience like in the workplace?
My first experience working in Los Angeles was absolutely phenomenal. I came on vacation to visit my sister Sandy. She and her husband, Tom Noonan, worked in the entertainment industry. By virtue of living with them on vacation, I determined that I would extend my stay after she asked me not to head back home. I looked for work. I worked with my brother Tommy at his offices in *Billboard Magazine*. That was a work environment that included not only every imaginable recording artist but also lots of other people who were associated with the entertainment industry. So it amazed me that what they were doing was called "work," because I had left an East Coast that was a much more formal environment.

What work experiences led you to see the need for a workplace-solutions company?
The failure to find an agency open to supporting my own career-search when I arrived in
Los Angeles more than forty years ago led me to identify how I would wish to be treated
as a job candidate. The experience I self-nurtured while managing an office in need of
rebuilding and staffing cemented for me that I had finally found my niche.

How did you transition from work in the entertainment industry to founding ActOne Group?
My work in the entertainment industry was not as an artist. When I was in entertainment,
I was managing an office. This helped me gain excellent experiences, skills and the visibility
to see what was missing in the support-staff arena.

**After coming up with the initial idea, what were some early steps you took to make
the ActOne Group a reality?**
The first thing I did was to ensure that I could operate from what I defined as a "good address."
Finding an area and neighborhoods ideally located for getting in contact with highly skilled
candidates with a lot of potential was a must for me early on. Being in close proximity to highly
skilled workers was not the only benefit, though. Another advantage of starting the business in
a safe place was that I could work long hours on my own and feel secure, and give candidates
a safe address to come to after-hours. This was necessary because, in those days, face-to-face
meetings were often a big part of the placement process. Skype didn't exist yet!

**When you made the jump to start your own company, what were some early obstacles
that you faced? How did you overcome them?**
The obstacle I faced in starting my company was not believing in myself enough to understand
that I actually could start a company. I didn't start my company from any particular perspective
of growing it into a multibillion-dollar organization, nor was I utilizing a lot of technology.
For a long time, the only technology I had was my phone. However, that also enabled me
to avoid a lot of obstacles as well because I truly was pioneering it.

"Never compromise who you are personally to become who you wish to become professionally."

Looking back, can you pinpoint one of your biggest mistakes as you built your company?
The biggest error of my career has been not forgiving myself for being smart, female, and African American at the same time. Lately, I've spoken a lot about this when mentoring because I find it is a common occurrence for women and minorities who are competing in a broad – and often global – marketplace.

And what were some of your best decisions you made during the early stages of starting up?
Understanding the importance of the candidate as the center of the universe and building all practices and protocols around this was then, as it is now, the single smartest decision I ever made.

If you were starting the founding process again today with all the wisdom you've accrued, is there anything you would do differently?
Because we are achieving phenomenal success as a privately owned company, I am pleased with our growth. Also, given that resources were limited in the founding years, organic growth versus VC or EP funding support would still be my first choice. The biggest "different" thing I'd possibly consider would be to invest in enterprise technology sooner. Today, off-the-shelf technologies solve many startup challenges; however, when I started my business, it was necessary to build our own technology in order to differentiate for competitiveness and efficiencies we sought.

What advice would you give to new founders starting out?
You should never compromise who you are personally to become who you wish to be professionally.

How has being based in Los Angeles influenced the mission statement and/or operations of the ActOne Group?
One of the ActOne Group's guiding principles is, "The applicant is the center of our universe." An educated, well-respected workforce is key to any business and critical to ours. The Greater Los Angeles area offers businesses some of the highest caliber employees anywhere in the USA and most of the world. The LA marketplace is as competitive as it is opportune.
A great business can do very well in Los Angeles. At the same time, to do well in Los Angeles, a business needs to be great in every way, and having the right talent is the first indicator of a company's ability to be great! In our company, we say "Everything matters." In Los Angeles, everything is available - everything that matters.

What do you envision for the future of ActOne Group and your own career?
ActOne Group will add European staffing offices over the next two years. We are currently in the process of upscaling the technology for many of our processes, which will disrupt how the job-placement process works, and just within the last two months, we've launched AllSTEM, a STEM placement firm dedicated to inclusion within the placement activities of companies who work with us. I'm also very excited about my newest book, *Acting Up: Winning in Business and Life Using Down-Home Wisdom*. It's available now on Amazon and Walmart online.

[About]   The ActOne Group provides employment, workforce management, and procurement solutions to a huge range of sectors, from Fortune 500 organizations to government agencies. Founded in 1978, the ActOne Group is a global business operating in over nineteen different countries and is the largest woman- and minority-owned, privately held workforce management firm in the US.

[Links]   Web: act1group.com Facebook: JaniceBryantHowroyd Twitter: @jbryanthowroyd
Instagram: jbryanthowroyd

What are your top work essentials?
iPad, iPhone, ideas!

At what age did you found your company?
Before thirty.

What's your most-used app?
Spotify.

**What's the most valuable piece of advice
you've been given?**
The result is the truth.

What's your greatest skill?
Discipline.

Nanxi Liu

Cofounder and CEO / Enplug, Inc.

Nanxi Liu is the cofounder and CEO of Enplug, Inc, a company that has modernized and simplified digital software for businesses around the world. Selected as a member of Forbes 30 Under 30, Nanxi created Enplug at age twenty-two just after graduating from UC Berkeley. While still an undergraduate, she cofounded and served as CEO of her first business, the biotech company Nanoly Bioscience, which developed a polymer that eliminates the need for refrigeration for vaccines and therapeutics. Originally from Colorado, she is a concert pianist and an advocate for STEM education for young women.

Tell me about your entrepreneurial path. How did you first get the idea to run a business?
My family and I came here as immigrants, so making money to support ourselves was crucial. As a kid, I would try to be creative in any way to make money. After I started learning piano, I signed up for competitions that had monetary rewards as a way to monetize my skill. In fifth grade, I then started teaching piano to kids in the neighborhood and then eventually posted ads up on Craigslist to expand my reach. That was my first step in running a business. In freshman year in college, I built computers chips that allowed lamps to turn on and off on campus based on how bright it was outside. Then I developed a mobile app for student safety that I showed the university. They gave me ten thousand dollars for it, which was pretty cool because it only took me maybe one weekend to build it. I always joke that every founder's rite of passage includes building a failed dating app, so of course, I too created a failed dating app.

Finally, during my senior year's winter break, I met my cofounder for my first company – a biotech company called Nanoly Bioscience. We met randomly at a bar and started talking, and I learned that he's a brilliant scientist. Immediately, I told him, "All right, let's start a company together and let's tackle the biggest problem we can think of in the world," which we felt like was healthcare. Together with several other scientists, we developed a polymer that eliminates refrigeration for vaccines and other temperature-sensitive therapeutics. All the failed little side projects I did in college led to finally being able to launch a product and know how to get a company funded.

I was serving as the CEO of Nanoly during my senior year of college. In between taking shots with my sorority sisters on Friday nights, I'd be applying for grants from the National Institute of Health. Soon after, I realized I do not have the expertise to run a biotech company. I had not taken a chemistry class since high school. I had my cofounder take over as CEO so I could start another company more in my background of software and tech. That's when Enplug was born.

Nanxi Liu / Enplug, Inc.

How did the idea for Enplug specifically emerge?

I love building products that solve problems. I care less than most about the initial idea and care more about the people and the possibilities. I think there are a lot of really good ideas out there, and each one's viability comes down to how effectively the people who are building it execute it. Basically, I'm not an ideas person; I'm a builder. For Enplug, I met smart, talented people who basically said, "We think that all the digital displays in the world should be easy to interact with and easy to control." We learned that it's extremely expensive and difficult to manage a network of digital displays with custom content. My cofounders and I believed that it should be simple and that even mom-and-pop shops should be able to have beautiful digital signage. We wanted to let businesses easily show employee engagement content, sales and marketing dashboards, menu boards and other custom content on screens. The market for digital signage is really big. We saw lots of companies in the industry that were very old. We looked at their software and saw it was severely outdated. Together as a team, we were excited to revolutionize digital signage software and have it accessible to all businesses. Because none of us came from the digital signage industry, we had a completely fresh, innovative design theory about what digital signage software should be. I'm proud that Enplug's made a major impact in modernizing the digital signage software industry.

What were some early challenges you faced? How did you overcome them?

In the early stages, it's always around the topic of "how are you going to fund a business?" This was especially relevant to us because we were building enterprise software. Our competitors had spent twenty years building their software, so we needed to do it in a fraction of the time and make our product better. We were all either college dropouts or recent graduates. We were these twenty-two and twenty-three-year-olds and really scrappy with how we spent money. The way we did it is by renting a one-bedroom, one-bathroom apartment in the Koreatown neighborhood of Los Angeles. We lived and worked out of this tiny place. The idea was to work like crazy and take no salary. We pooled together our money to pay for the food, which was lots of ramen and cereal, and then we would just work. Even after we got some outside funding, we kept that mentality of trying to reserve our cash. So we upgraded and rented a house, this time in Bel Air, where at one point we had thirteen people living and working together under one roof. We quickly outgrew the house and moved into a real office building, which now serves as our headquarters. Today, we have global offices around the world. But it all started out by all of us diving right in and collaborating as both coworkers and roommates.

" *Don't ask other people for validation on your idea. Just start building it yourself.* "

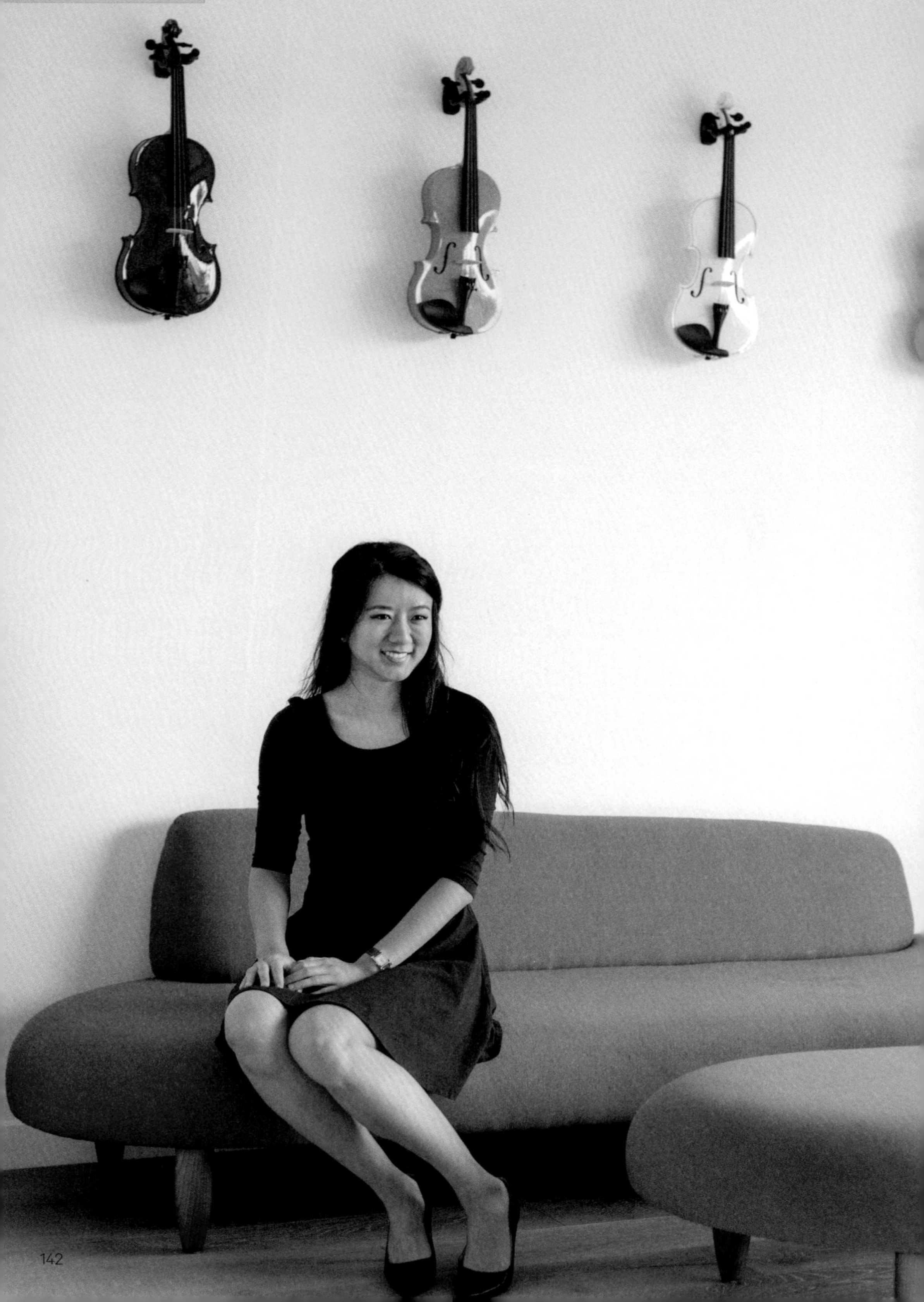

Looking back at your first stages of starting up, what would you characterize as your best decision?

The best decision has been who we brought on as teammates. Because we didn't have a lot of money in the early days, our pitch to potential hires was that we would cover their room and board and we'd give them a small stipend. The fact that we had incredibly talented people across many fields – engineering, design, sales – all willing to forgo high-paying, stable jobs to instead join us reflected strongly on their commitment and their own vision of building a great tech company together.

What would pinpoint as your biggest mistake?

I think my biggest mistake was setting unrealistic expectations for myself and the team in our early days. I thought it would be possible to become a billion-dollar company in just a few years. That's incredibly rare, especially in enterprise software. Our unattainably high goal led to disappointment and made it feel like we were constantly failing when in actuality we were growing quite quickly for a SaaS company. If I were to go back in time, I would create better-calibrated goals so that we celebrated the progress we were making.

What advice would you give to new founders starting up?

Don't ask other people for validation on your idea. Dive in and start building it yourself. Believe in yourself and your capabilities. Know what you're really good at and apply those strengths to your pursuit. Third, find people that are really strong in areas that complement your skills. Finally, both written and verbal communication are extremely important. You have to be able to sell the idea of the product and company whether to clients or investors or potential hires.

What does being based in Los Angeles bring to Enplug?

I grew up in Colorado, went to college at UC Berkeley and had my biotech company up in the Bay Area, but I wanted to build Enplug in Los Angeles. When I first chose to move to LA, I didn't have any other reason to be here except that my cofounders were here. As we built Enplug, I realized I wouldn't want to be anywhere else. LA is the best city I could ever want to build a company. There's a huge talent pool because we are surrounded by some of the top education institutions in the world. People have a better work–life balance here, enabling us to be more productive and creative. The LA environment offers a huge variety of activities – the beach, nature – and a diverse group of people that make it enriching to live here. We get to be exposed to lots of different industries and people. It's a very close-knit startup community because everyone's trying to build the city into a great entrepreneurial hub. San Francisco is established and feels like a more competitive environment than LA, where it feels very nurturing. All the founders here want to help each other. People want to support building and growing the business community. Compared to NY and SF, LA is also a way more affordable place to operate and start a company.

What's something about Enplug that you want people to know?

Our team, my CTO, Justyna Denuit-Wojcik, and I are really involved in mentoring, supporting and advocating for women to pursue entrepreneurship and for girls to study STEM. We're really passionate about this work and are volunteers at many organizations that focus on giving more opportunities to women. Justyna and I have firsthand experience on the many more obstacles women face in starting our own companies and working in the tech industry. That's why we feel that much more responsible to make sure we do everything we can to support women pursuing entrepreneurship and technology.

[About] Enplug is a globally operating digital-signage software company. The software enables companies to manage and distribute custom content on screens for marketing and communications.

[Links] Web: **enplug.com** Facebook: **Enplug** Twitter: **@Enplug** Instagram: **enplug**

What are your top work essentials?
Phone, laptop, Internet.

At what age did you found your company?
Twenty-two.

What's your most-used app?
Gmail.

**What's the most valuable piece of advice
you've been given?**
You are the average of the five people you spend
the most time with.

What's your greatest skill?
Problem-solving.

Natasha Case

CEO and Cofounder / Coolhaus

Los Angeles native, Natasha Case, received her Masters of Architecture degree from UCLA, and began interning at Walt Disney Imagineering in Hotel and Master Planning. During this time, she started baking cookies, making ice cream, and combining them into "cool houses" with co-founder and wife Freya Estreller. Today, Coolhaus is the leading women owned ice cream brand in the country and distributes in 7,500+ grocery stores ranging from Whole Foods to Safeway to Publix markets including hand-crafted premium ice cream sandwiches, artisan pints and chocolate-dipped bars. Natasha works as CEO, creating new products, designing packaging, leading marketing, and innovating ideas.

Tell me about your entrepreneurial path. You come from an architecture background – what made you decide to try starting a business?
I always thought about architecture as something I was really passionate about, but at the same time, I saw a broader application for it and a chance to learn the rules and then break them apart. That definitely segues into entrepreneurial thinking, but I wasn't deliberately thinking about that path. When the recession hit, I was working at Disney Imagineering, which was my first job after seven years of architecture school. I had already been experimenting with "food meets design" and was calling it "farchitecture." Under this concept umbrella, I started baking cookies and making ice cream and naming the combinations after architects. I'd give them to people at work who had gotten bad news to lighten the mood or as comic relief. Someone maybe had been laid off or heard something they didn't want to hear, and I'd say "Here's a Mies Vanilla Rohe or Mintimalism." It was a very passionate hobby and a way to do certain things with design but definitely not think of it in a traditional way. Then I met Freya, the other founder. She had a little bit more business background and saw the business potential in the idea. That's when we really started thinking of it in that way: putting numbers to it and going through the cost of goods. She turned on that light.

What were some of the first challenges you faced in those early stages of starting up?
We had such humble beginnings – we had nothing to work with in terms of dollars, and because of the recession, we weren't going to get a bank loan. People were not looking to throw around money into investments, and we were young and didn't have much to show for ourselves from a business front. So we had to do everything and figure out absolutely everything on our own.

Freya and I also started dating right when we started the business. That definitely creates an interesting foundation, because you're learning to run a business of ice-cream sandwiches but also learning who each other is. There's a lot of unknowns. You're figuring out how you're going to work together and how you're going to be a couple. Many people could have told us that we were heading for a disaster by throwing all the eggs in that basket. But sometimes you just know and it works out. I think that was a combination of luck and instinct. Business resources were also much more scarce. We had to just figure things out with cold searches online or by cold-calling people and asking them how they did it. Now, there's coworking spaces and millions of panels and events and conferences fully dedicated to that startup experience and so much more awareness about it. I like that we came from none of that, because I think in some ways entrepreneurship has become over-glamorized. But it definitely did not not make it easier. I also certainly experienced ageism: people just being like, "Oh you're a twenty-five-year-old kid. You have no clue." So we had to constantly believe in our idea.

How would you characterize what success means to you now?

We want to be the household brand of our generation. Specifically, there's an incredible opportunity to do that as a culture of women leadership. That's going to be very meaningful for our generation, to be a powerhouse of women who are behind that brand, who created and are very involved in that thought process. Although I think we'll have to eventually break out of even the freezer aisle, I think there's a massive opportunity in the novelty world. Most of the premium brands that really represent today's culture of what people want from ice cream are creating really exciting pints. And that's still worth a lot. Innovating and making full time is a lot of work, and you still don't see those premium brands really touching the novelty part of the ice-cream category because it's almost doubly difficult. It's about doing unique flavors made really well. But you also have to think about: Am I going to create a whole new novelty? Am I going to reinvent something that involves cookies and cones? There are all these other facets to it. So I think we could completely take over and be the quality, the brand and the voice that people are looking for. Ultimately, we're interested in a strategic exit. So I think it's something we could very much bring to the table for a multinational strategic partner.

Looking back, can you pinpoint any mistakes or things you might have done differently?

I don't look at the mistakes as needing to do them differently, because I think you need those mistakes to come to certain realizations. As long as you come to them quickly and, in entrepreneurial terms, fail forward, it's totally fine. For example, we opened a truck operation in Miami. It made a lot of sense. We were basically snowboarding our trucks from New York down to Miami because their summer is the opposite of New York's. And we did grow awareness and learned a whole other market; however, ultimately it was really difficult to remotely manage a business in Miami, so we had to pull the cord. But I'm proud of how quickly we did it. Also, we had built a lot of awareness down there, and now our grocery business is quite strong. That's connected to the fact that we had the trucks there for a year or so.

" *We want to be the household brand of our generation. Specifically, there's an incredible opportunity to do that as a culture of women leadership.* "

What's something you still consider a strong decision?

The way that we started to focus on grocery as a major potential winner. We started as a truck business. Then, in 2012, we decided to re-examine a couple of channels we hadn't had the opportunity to in the early days, which was brick-and-mortar shops and grocery. We opened our flagship store in Culver City, but we also did a test with Whole Foods. They were amazing partners, but I don't think we really treated and saw the Whole Foods business as the potential business we now see it. Wholesale is really tough when you're a little guy. You're getting less margin, you don't really have all the scalability built in. But now we've fine-tuned our business to lend itself towards scaling there. We can't have a truck, and we can't have a shop in every city, but we can be everyone's hometown ice-cream brand by being able to be at their local grocery store shelf.

What advice would you give to founders starting out, especially to those who are women or part of demographics that are underrepresented among entrepreneurs?

The most honest answer is, if I'd have known how hard and crazy it would be to put on an annual conference and do the work at the magnitude of what we've done, I don't know if I'd have done it. Just to be honest, right? It's a lot, and it takes a big emotional and personal toll, even with all the success we've had. It's just kind of the nature of everything that we've done. So if I'd have known that, I may not have continued to go down that road or pursued the idea. And I would relate that answer to starting Space Called Tribe – the amount of time and work that it took to get the building going, to continue to fill it and support entrepreneurs, and even be in a city that's so, so underestimated… it's a lot to carry.

What professional advice would you give people in the early stages of starting out?

Visioning is really important. It could be a journal, it could be a Pinterest board, but map out what the two-, five- and ten-year mark looks like to your business and looks like for you. I think we women don't factor ourselves into the equation enough, often thinking about everybody else instead, so you need to know at the two-, five- and ten-year marks, are you going to be making enough money from this business? Are you going to feel burned out? What's your role going to be? Just taking the time to think really, really big.

How has being Los Angeles–based influenced your company?

Hugely. There are a number of factors. People don't think of entertainment this way, but it really is an industry built by bohemians and artists. It's a creative industry. So LA is not built as a nine-to-five, and that that lends itself really well to the entrepreneurial setting and lifestyle. Another thing is that I call LA almost like a rehab for New Yorkers. You have a lot of that big-city and New York energy here, but it's also mellowed by the fact that it's a warm climate, and that it's the West Coast. It's a little more chill. I've found it to be a really good workforce. You have driven people who are hungry, but they also want to be balanced and have fun and enjoy what they're doing. It's not this insanely over-competitive environment. We also started with trucks: LA is pretty nice so you can run a truck business year-round here. It's a car culture, so people really notice your ice-cream truck. It looks cool on the freeway.

LA is also a city that's continuing to figure itself out. That's an exciting place for entrepreneurs. Now, you have so much tech business coming down here. It's becoming much more multifaceted than just being about Hollywood. LA is so hugely influential to why we are the way that we are.

[About]　Coolhaus aims to be the next household name for ice cream. With origins as a food-truck operation, it has since expanded to two brick-and-mortar shops and a grocery business nationwide.

　[Links]　Web: cool.haus Facebook: Coolhaus Twitter: @COOLHAUS Instagram: coolhaus

What are your top work essentials?
Reusable water bottle, matcha green tea, good sunglasses, strong lip color.

At what age did you found your company?
Twenty-five.

What's your most-used app?
Boomerang for Gmail.

What's the most valuable piece of advice you've been given?
You can walk through a wall when you don't know it's there. So, a perceived obstacle can actually be your biggest gift.

What's your greatest skill?
Inspiring people.

Shivani Siroya

Founder and CEO / Tala

Shivani Siroya is the founder and CEO of Tala, the leading consumer-lending app in emerging markets. She previously held a variety of positions in global health, microfinance and investment banking, including with the United Nations Population Fund, Health Net, Citigroup and UBS. Shivani is an Aspen Institute Finance Leader Fellow, a WEF Young Global Leader, Senior TED Fellow and Ashoka Fellow. She is also on the board of Stellar.org. She holds an MPH from Columbia University and a BA from Wesleyan University.

What was the genesis of the idea for Tala?

When I worked at the UN Population Fund, I had the opportunity to interview over 3,500 individuals across nine different markets in West Africa and sub-Saharan Africa. I realized that access to credit was not just a problem in one country but across the board. It was a foundational infrastructure issue. People weren't getting access to credit, savings or other financial products because we didn't have the data on these customers to be able to understand their creditworthiness. Many times, we were missing a national ID, we didn't have a credit score, and we didn't understand what they were doing with the capital, or what they wanted to do or should do. We didn't understand their daily life or true financial life.

I realized there were ways for us to gain that data-understanding and develop a relationship with the customer to build that financial ecosystem. A lot of the data can be gathered through our mobile phones and through our own application. By doing thousands of interviews and living in those markets, I really viscerally understood the creditworthiness of the customer. The second piece was realizing there's a potential way to solve this problem, and it's not by just giving people money; it's by actually solving the underlying root causes and infrastructure problems that exist in financial systems in emerging markets. That solves the system-wide problem and not just the product-access problem

What were your initial steps in moving from idea to startup?

I left the UN and started working in investment banking again. I couldn't forget about this problem. I ended up emailing 1,500 people on LinkedIn, trying to find anybody else that was trying to solve it. As I talked to more mentors and advisors, people really told me, "Nobody's solving this; you should do it." It made me realize there was a hole in the industry. The first piece I always go to is: You have to identify a problem. You have to be proximate to the problem to understand the pain point your customers are feeling.

The second piece is knowing, does another solution exist? You don't want to bring something to the market that's redundant, especially when you're thinking about solving system problems. It's not just about creating a better-quality product; it's actually about solving that underlying issue.

The next part is, how do I actually do this? I didn't know a thing about the startup world or venture capital. I ended up learning how to code on the side and building our prototype and actually using my savings to test our models. I worked full time. A mentor of mine told me, "You've never done this. As a woman, you need to be independent. You need to be able to actually care for yourself through this process." She told me that unless I had six to twelve months of rent in the bank, I could not quit my job. So I didn't. Then, when I was having conversations with investors, things moved very quickly, because I understood why our solution was different, why this would work, what the problem was, the market opportunity. And I could come in with a lot more confidence.

What were some early struggles you encountered, and how did you overcome them?
One early one was the decision to do our own lending. Initially, when we started, our solution was about building a relationship with the customer. We'd work within these markets and get customers to download our application. The second piece was we would use their data, with their permission, and actually create credit scores for them and work with banks to help them gain access to credit. But it was slow. A challenge was feeling frustrated – we've developed these credit scores that we feel confident in, we feel like our customers are creditworthy, and yet they're still not being treated well. So the challenge was feeling like you haven't solved the problem.

We decided to do a 180 and prove to the market that these customers were creditworthy. The best way to do that was to actually own our own destiny and own the entire value chain. So we went to our board and we said, "We're going to go use our own capital to test the models and show the market that we're right." We overcame that challenge by trusting our gut and being willing to take the first risk.

" Be willing to take the risk, because otherwise why are any of us doing this? Let's not play safe. "

Looking back, is there anything you wish you'd known before jumping in or that you might have done differently?

As a small, scrappy startup, so many people are willing to join at that stage because they're generalists. They're willing to do anything you need and everyone's all hands on deck. As you grow, you need to start thinking about specialization. You need to be thinking about the different tracks of work and skill you'll need in the long term. Something I wish I'd known is to prepare for that a bit earlier – think through the timing of those specialists coming in, how we're going to recruit them – having my eye on that a little earlier to develop those relationships. I think that's something we don't all talk about. We're always talking about thinking one round ahead, making sure you raise more money than you need right now, but I think a lot of this is actually that people make really successful companies.

How has being Los Angeles–based influenced Tala?

It's been great for us. We're not in a bubble. We're not sitting in Silicon Valley. We're not sitting in New York. We have this amazing environment that promotes a very healthy attitude. There's no distraction by the competitive nature of the other startups around you. We keep our heads down, we can stay humble and focused on the problem we're solving and develop an internal culture that's really strong. I think the community around us is also incredibly supportive because we each want each other to succeed. Because it's a new emerging community in a sense, everyone is super excited about every startup that gets funded in Santa Monica or LA. It means that all the boats rise up together. I've noticed great references coming from other companies. We pass each other referrals. We talk about different investors and bring investors to each other's companies.

I think the challenge is that LA is an emerging community. In that sense, the city itself is changing around the startup scene as well. We're starting to see a lot of folks move here from San Francisco and New York independently of job offers, just wanting to move their families for their own work–life balance. Earlier on, it was a challenge getting people to realize that, hey, if you move to LA and things don't work out at Tala, there is still a ton of other really great companies here. Sometimes people felt like it was too big of a risk to move, which I think is now changing.

What advice would you give entrepreneurs in the early stages of starting up?

Understand your customers and the issues affecting them. If you can walk in their shoes and really understand what problem you're solving and internalize what that pain point is, then a solution will come about. You may adjust that solution multiple times, but you're on the path to it because you've at least been able to internalize what you're solving for. You've got that awareness and empathy for the problem. I think a lot of people jump to the solutions or jump to the fact that they want to start a company before actually knowing what the company would be.

What do you look back on as your biggest mistake?

I came into this saying we really want to have a systemic level of impact. We want to actually change an entire system globally. If that's the case, then we should have been bolder from the starting point. Now we own that entire value chain and we're fixing the whole thing piece by piece. When we started, we thought we only needed to fix a portion of it to actually have that system impact. A mistake is not being bold. I would tell others, you're taking on a global problem – be bold about it. Be willing to take the risk, because otherwise why are any of us doing this? Let's not play safe.

What about your best decision?

Every year that goes by, we push our vision even farther. That's been really exciting and successful. We are relentless in that pursuit and constantly challenging our limits. I'm really proud of that, because it tells me that we're not just doing the thing, but the how of how we're doing it has become just as important to us.

What are you particularly excited about regarding Tala right now?

From the outside, it can look like we're just a financial-services company or a lending company, but we have fundamentally had to create the entire financial stack to actually do what we do. Everything from thinking about how you identify someone to how you actually score them and how you service them. There's a large component of infrastructure along with software. That's the thing I would mention: when you talk to companies or when we talk to each other, how do we get at the deeper stuff that companies are actually solving instead of what we put out there as headlines.

[About]   Tala is an app that provides credit to those without a traditional credit history. Through its own application system, Tala scores users who are usually excluded from opportunities via credit bureaus to provide them the financial agency to build their futures.

[Links]   Web: tala.co Facebook: talamobile Twitter: @talamobile Instagram: talamobile

What are your top work essentials?
Laptop, thirty-two-ounce water bottle, notebook.

At what age did you found your company?
Twenty-seven..

What's your most-used app?
Gmail.

What's the most valuable piece of advice you've been given?
Listen and learn. Be curious and constantly be open to change.

What's your greatest skill?
My ability to believe in people.

ools

- **Be passionate.**
  You should have passion in your medium or area
  of study, and this passion should be evident in your
  portfolio. Our admissions counselors are available
  to guide applicants preparing portfolios prior
  to admission.

- **We want open-minded students.**
  You should have a desire to ask questions and
  interrogate the world.

- **See yourself as an agent of change.**
  You should see art and design as a tool to foster
  change and make the world a better place.

- **Be eager to learn.**
  You should be receptive to different ideas and have
  a willingness to try new things, experiment, take
  risks and fail.

[Name]

ArtCenter College of Design

[Elevator Pitch]

"Entrepreneurship is in ArtCenter's DNA. We provide a broad foundation in business and entrepreneurship for our students, which is complemented by a hands-on learning approach in studio classes. Students are tasked to solve real problems under conditions designed to replicate what they will experience in their future professional careers."

[Enrollment]

2,100 students (2018)

[Description]

ArtCenter is educating the next generation of artists and designers to influence change by aligning rigorous creative education with business and entrepreneurship acumen. Complementing this coursework is a program called BOLD, a series of symposia, workshops and seminars focused on propelling creative entrepreneurs. "We are leading the field in our unique integration of startup strategy, business management and research offerings within the traditional fields of design and visual arts," says Robbie Nock, director of ArtCenter's Entrepreneurship and Professional Practice program. "We see a significant and expanding role for creatives within startups and established organizations. It is critical for us to provide this broader toolkit and educational experience that shapes artists and designers into leaders and visionaries that can adapt to changing industries."

ArtCenter, located in Pasadena, offers degrees across eleven undergraduate and seven graduate programs. For those interested in pursuing entrepreneurship, there are over seventy-five unique classes across the college. Classes are designed to serve as a runway where students have the opportunity to apply their creative visions by learning strategy, team building, market research, customer acquisition and finance. When graduating, students can apply for Launch Lab, a capstone program that provides a tuition-free term with access to up to $5,000 in equity-free capital for use in finalizing business plans and preparing for the next steps. ArtCenter alumni have founded numerous startups and work for some of the most influential companies in the world, including Airbnb, Amazon, Apple, Disney, Google, Lyft, Microsoft, Nike and Tesla. "Students here get the skillset and hands-on experience they need within a responsive educational context," Robbie says. "We invite them to take risks and fail often so that they can learn to be comfortable with the uncertainty that exists in the rapidly changing startup and business landscape. As agents of change, our students graduate prepared to tackle the significant problems facing our world today."

[Apply to]   artcenter.edu/apply.html

[Links]   Web: artcenter.edu   Facebook: artcenteredu   Twitter: @artcenteredu   Instagram: artcenteredu

- **Have energy and drive, and exhibit a passion for learning.**
  There's a reason Cal State LA is ranked number one in the nation for the upward mobility of its students. Our students don't take educational opportunities for granted, and they are focused and motivated to achieve their goals.

- **Take the lead.**
  Cal State LA students study but also innovate. They display leadership qualities and possess the ability to execute creative ideas.

- **Have a desire to give back.**
  The college experience is about more than holing up in the library. Academics are important, but so is community.

- **Display good communication skills.**
  Vital campus discourse is buoyed by students who clearly convey their thoughts and ideas.

- **Be able to think critically.**
  Critical thinking is a valuable skill across areas of study, whether analyzing a novel or creating a new piece of technology. For Cal State LA students, critical problem-solving skills are essential.

[Name]
Cal State LA

[Elevator Pitch]
"Ranked number one in the nation for the upward mobility of our students, we provide life-changing education for a diverse student body. Our Entrepreneurship Option within the Bachelor of Science in Business Administration degree and Cal State LA BioSpace Initiative offer specific opportunities for founders to make their mark."

[Enrollment]
28,000 (2019)

[Description]
Cal State LA draws on the entrepreneurial spirit. As evidenced by its ranking as number one in the nation for the upward mobility of its students, the LA-based public university attracts students eager to innovate and make their marks on the world. For those looking to build business-specific skills within their course of study, the school offers an Entrepreneurship Option within the Bachelor of Science in Business Administration degree. Still, the school emphasizes that students across all disciplines will experience a course of study infused with entrepreneurial ethos. Cal State LA is focused on providing resources for ambitious students to actualize their goals.

Both undergraduates and local founders interested in launching ventures in the bioscience fields will find opportunity through Cal State LA BioSpace, which is leading the University's mission to promote a thriving bioscience ecosystem in the heart of LA. Developed with investment from the Los Angeles County Board of Supervisors, the Economic Development Administration (EDA) of the U.S. Department of Commerce, and philanthropic support, the initiative includes the creation of the 20,000 ft^2 (1,858 m^2) on-campus Rongxiang Xu Bioscience Innovation Center, where entrepreneurs will find lab spaces and resources vital to launching ventures.

The initiative includes an incubator housed within the center. This fills a vital need for bioscience resources for emerging entrepreneurs from underserved communities while also offering a unique opportunity for university engagement with these communities. Participating entrepreneurs, students and faculty can learn from each other while taking advantage of the provided coworking space, classrooms, and wet, dry and specialized labs. Cal State LA BioSpace also offers Cal State LA BioStart, a five-week intensive training program for emerging bioscience entrepreneurs. Over the course of the training, industry specialists impart education on business, marketing and leadership skills to help participants move toward launching their own bioscience startups. The program is provided to eligible participants free of cost.

[Apply to]
www2.calstate.edu/apply

[Links]
Web: **calstatela.edu** Facebook: **CalStateLA** Twitter: **@calstatela** Instagram: **calstatela**

- **Be entrepreneurial minded.**
  We want students who have a passion for wanting to make a difference in this world through entrepreneurship.

- **Want to fix issues.**
  The best students are the ones who don't just want to make money but also want to find solutions to societal issues.

- **Problem-solving skills are a must.**
  Wanting to fix issues is important, but so is knowing how to fix issues. We want students who can think of creative solutions to solve problems. We will help you develop this mindset.

- **Be service oriented.**
  As a Jesuit school, we want students who appreciate the idea of service and social justice. We want this to be reflected in our students' cocurricular activities.

- **Get involved before coming to campus.**
  We do a lot of high school programs in the area. If you are serious about going to LMU, come take part in one of our events.

[Name]

Loyola Marymount University

[Elevator Pitch]

"Loyola Marymount University offers rigorous undergraduate, graduate and professional programs to academically ambitious students committed to lives of meaning and purpose."

[Enrollment]

6,000 (2019)

[Description]

Since its founding by Jesuits in 1911, Loyola Marymount University has sought to instill a passion for education, faith, justice and social impact in students of diverse talents, interests and backgrounds. Today that mission is applied across sixty different majors within six colleges and schools: Liberal Arts, Science and Engineering, Communication and Fine Arts, Education, Film and Television, and Business Administration. LMU's campus is located in the heart of Silicon Beach, the Westside region of Los Angeles that is home to over five hundred tech companies, including Facebook, Google, Yahoo!, Snap, and Hulu. LMU has long-standing strategic relationships and industry partnerships within this ecosystem, and it opened a new campus in Playa Vista in 2018 to better position the university for global imagination and impact.

LMU's Fred Kiesner Center for Entrepreneurship, one of the oldest entrepreneurship schools in the country, boasts a faculty of seasoned entrepreneurs, many of whom run public companies, sit on the board of a company or have started their own business. "We believe you cannot teach students how to be entrepreneurs unless you have gone through the struggles of starting and running your own business," says Darlene Fukuji, associate director of the Fred Kiesner Center for Entrepreneurship.

Undergraduate tuition at LMU costs $48,000 annually. LMU also offers a business incubator program every semester, which provides students with the resources they need to turn a business idea into a reality. "We give students a workspace and access to experts, alumni, entrepreneurs and investors to help them launch their business," says Fukuji. "At any one time, we have at least a dozen businesses being incubated in our program." LMU's graduates have gone on to generate about $1 billion in revenues every year and have sold about $1 billion worth of businesses. This is one of the reasons LMU is ranked eleventh in the US in entrepreneurship, according to *U.S. News and World Report*.

[Apply to]

lmu.edu/admission

[Links]

Web: **lmu.edu** Facebook: **lmula** Twitter: **@LoyolaMarymount** Instagram: **loyolamarymount**

- **Demonstrate high levels of academic prowess and the potential to continue to improve.**
  Most students admitted into USC are in the top 10 percent of their graduating class, with median standardized test scores in the top 5 percent.

- **Prepare for your intended majors.**
  USC pays close attention to your preparations. Ensure your academic and extracurricular record highlights what you're interested in studying and be prepared to submit a portfolio or attend an audition for specific majors.

- **Have impact potential.**
  In your application, demonstrate your potential to make an impact as a future learning and research partner at USC and show your desire to exceed requirements, explore new ideas and be a lifelong learner.

- **Be a community player.**
  USC strives to enroll a diverse student body representing many different perspectives and passions. Show us how you will enrich the experiences of other students, challenge your peers and contribute to the campus community.

[Name]
USC (University of Southern California)

[Elevator Pitch]
"We are a leading private research university in Los Angeles, a global center for arts, business and technology. We have exceptional academic schools and units, and we are LA's largest private employer, responsible for $8 billion in annual economic activity."

[Enrollment]
47,500 (2018–2019)

[Description]
USC opened its doors in 1880, nearly a decade after founder Judge Robert Maclay Widney decided to set up a university on an unpaved area of early Los Angeles. The school, built on land given to Widney by community leaders in 1879, started with only fifty-three students and ten faculty members. Nearly a century and a half later, USC has become a leading research university, with a huge array of undergraduate and graduate programs, a highly ranked medical center and a growing focus on innovation.

To honor the risk Widney took in founding USC while what would become Los Angeles was still a small pueblo (town), the university is committed to producing academically and ethically strong graduates. As the university's 2018 strategic plan states, "To lead in this area is to fashion and support a culture of creativity, engagement, impact, and entrepreneurship (CEIE) across our campuses." USC upholds innovative values by creating entrepreneurship policies, reworking how students measure their success and impact, and baking CEIE into curricular and extracurricular programs and activities. From the Women In Science and Engineering (WISE) program to the Media Communications Lab, USC has a wide offering of labs and programs for students of all backgrounds, strengths and curiosities.

One of the main entrepreneurship programs USC offers is the Blackstone Launchpad, part of the Lloyd Greif Center for Entrepreneurial Studies at the USC Marshall School of Business. Open to all students and alumni, the campus-based incubator gives participants mentoring, networking opportunities, and access to resources to accelerate their business. More than 10 percent of USC's student population is enrolled in the Blackstone Launchpad, with millions of dollars of capital investment awarded to USC-backed ventures from the VC community every year. USC students and grads have produced companies like Riot Games, Salesforce, Tinder and Bird, and today's students are working on new companies in industries from social media to gaming to health and wellness. Average tuition for USC students is $55,000 a year.

[Apply to]
admit.usc.edu

[Links]
Web: **usc.edu; incubate.usc.edu** Facebook: **usc** Twitter: **@USCMarshall** Instagram: **uscedu**

stors

IN THE FUT
ELECTRIC (
COULD POW
THE GRID

When you plug in your electri
flows from the grid to charge
But what if that electricity als
other way, from the charged b
the grid? Then the electricity
car battery could help out the
high demand. This isn't happe
on the horizon.

- **Have a company run by women and people of color.**
  We have a mission to expand opportunities in the tech
  and startup world for underrepresented populations.
  We specifically invest in manufacturing companies
  run by women and people of color that have not yet
  expanded into international exports.

- **Have existing cash flow.**
  We typically partner with already-existing companies
  as opposed to true startups. We look for enterprises
  with domestic cash flow and jump in to help initiate
  the addition of foreign exports.

- **Create the jobs of the future.**
  We're interested in investing in women and people
  of color in markets like cleantech and sustainability,
  ensuring representation in the fields that are creating
  jobs of the future.

- **Focus on social impact.**
  Women are about 1.17 percent more likely to start a
  social-impact company. Aligning with our mission-based
  values, we value partnering with enterprises that have
  goals for cultural change.

[Name] # The 22 Fund

[Elevator Pitch] *"We invest to increase the export capacity of manufacturing companies. Our mission is to create jobs of the future in underserved communities and invest in women and people-of-color entrepreneurs."*

[Sector] **Manufacturing**

[Description] In her first role at a venture capital firm, Tracy Gray saw millions in funds allocated to white male entrepreneurs. Years later, she founded The 22 Fund, a growth-equity and advisory firm whose mission is to bring women and people of color into the Los Angeles tech community and create quality jobs in underserved communities. The 22 Fund specifically backs existing manufacturing companies run by women and people of color to help expand exports, essentially funding the creation of an international sales unit startup within an already cash-flowing enterprise. This focus on the manufacturing industry aligned with Tracy's background in engineering and her interest in hard tech, and she also knew from her previous job as a senior adviser to the Mayor of Los Angeles for International Business that it was a strong and overlooked opportunity for investment. Los Angeles is the country's largest region for exports, and companies with international exports are 44 percent more successful and create jobs with higher wages. The 22 Fund walks companies through what can be an obfuscated process toward exporting, connecting them with overseas partners that can help them understand the international markets they'll enter, and advising them on domestic regulations for internationally exporting American companies.

The focus on manufacturing also allows for the seamless fulfillment of The 22 Fund's goal to create the jobs of the future in underserved communities, since manufacturing companies traditionally headquarter in lower-income areas for access to cheaper land, creating work opportunities for local residents. The 22 Fund values social impact on myriad levels, with a mission to change the systemically exclusionary investment system and make the world a better place. Its focus on women founders and founders of color provides funding to those typically excluded from venture capital, generating opportunities for wealth-building among marginalized communities. In addition to her role as the founder and managing partner of The 22 Fund, Tracy also founded the nonprofit We Are Enough, which aims to increase the number of women globally making investments in women-owned businesses and/or investing with a gender lens on the public markets.

[Apply to] the22fund.com/apply-to-the-22-2

[Links] Web: **the22fund.com**

- **Be ready for growth.**
  We look to invest in companies that are ready for growth and ready to use a mix of corporate and entrepreneurial strategies to move toward their next iteration.

- **Seek opportunities for transformation.**
  Is your company looking to undergo a transformation? We work with enterprises looking to change strategy from within to move their business in a new direction.

- **Be ready to disrupt.**
  We partner with companies ready to disrupt the traditional modes of operation in their sector. Are you ready to fundamentally alter the way a type of business or transaction is done in our culture?

- **Be interested in creating a portfolio.**
  We work with companies who are interested in creating their own portfolio of businesses to operate as a type of venture capitalist themselves.

[Name] # BCG Digital Ventures

[Elevator Pitch] *"We build game-changing, disruptive, white-space businesses that don't exist today."*

[Sector] **Sector agnostic**

[Description] BCG Digital Ventures is an investment firm that operates in tandem with consulting management firm Boston Consulting Group. It invests alongside corporations in emerging startups, giving large, established companies the opportunity to be key players in the next stage of technological innovation. This type of unique investment fills a previous gap within the wider BCG portfolio. The firm works with companies across verticals, and its partnership opportunities primarily come through its relationship with BCG proper. BCG Digital Ventures begins work with a client by gaining a thorough understanding of the details of the business: why it exists, who makes up its customer base, what makes it unique in market and what its products are. Operating with a unique blend of corporate resources, expertise and entrepreneurial ethos, it assesses the business for pain points or areas of friction and devises a personalized strategy to help with growth or reinvention. The investment firm stands out for its pacing: they can move from concept to launch in twelve months. Businesses looking for immediate transformation benefit from the partnership and see growth gains without experiencing a drawn-out trial-and-error process that would otherwise last years. In just a short amount of time, BCG Digital Ventures helps to rebrand or disrupt a long-established company, or it works with it to invest in new innovations, helping to bring the corporation into the future.

BCG Digital Ventures values capitalizing on startup opportunities to improve society. By connecting major companies with emerging disruptors, they're able to unite business interests in pursuit of common transformative goals. They look to partner with companies interested in growth, change, disruption and developing their own roster of portfolio businesses. "Our Global IP and Investment team is responsible for making strategic investments into our business that drive growth," says Eyana Carballo, the global commercial strategy and IP manager. Companies within the BCG Digital Ventures portfolio include AutoGravity, a technology that revolutionizes the car-buying experience, and Endpoint, which makes the home-closing process simple, fast and transparent.

[Apply to] **bcgdv.com**

[Links] Web: **bcgdv.com** Facebook: **BCGDV** Twitter: **@BCGDV** Instagram: **BCGDV**

- **Have boots on the ground. We like people who have been in the field.** They see a unique opportunity to leverage technology to improve efficiency, create better outcomes, lower costs and so on.

- **Show some traction.**
  Usually, we come in once a company has product-market fit and we're able to pour fuel on the fire in terms of sales and marketing. There are exceptions to every rule, and we have some preproduct investments and later-stage bets, but generally, we like to see product-market fit.

- **Have a strong management team.**
  We like to see domain expertise in our founders.

- **Do something new.**
  One thing that's exciting is how our mix of investments has changed and evolved with the tech ecosystem. We're always interested in investing in new categories, in new areas that are being created.

- **Have LA roots.**
  We're really excited to invest in entrepreneurs that are born and bred in LA.

[Name]

Crosscut Ventures

[Elevator Pitch]

"We partner with early-stage founders to build extraordinary high-growth tech companies from seed to Series A."

[Sector]

Multiple

[Description]

Over a decade ago, Crosscut Ventures made a bet, not in a technology but in a city. That city was Los Angeles, and many companies and four funds later, that bet – despite having been wagered just around the time of the 2008 financial downturn – seems to have paid off. Now a well-established venture fund, Crosscut Ventures has not forgotten its local roots in the LA ecosystem. "The investments we've made in the last ten years really track the LA ecosystem," says Maureen Klewicki, a senior associate at Crosscut Ventures. "We've been all-in on LA for a long time, and we've seen the ecosystem develop and grow, and now it really feels like it's at an inflection point where we have talent coming out of companies that were started here and raised funding here."

As a generalist fund, Crosscut Ventures has invested across a wide range of industries, from mobility and esports to space and other frontier investments. In addition to its typical investments, which range from $1.5 million to $2.5 million at the seed round, Crosscut Ventures also reserves 200 percent of its initial investment for follow-on capital.

The fund, which is run by a team of investors who all come from operational backgrounds, including former founders, lawyers and executives, also aims to support startups in other ways, such as through a wide network of industry experts and deep connections to local players in the ecosystem. And, as a locally founded and based fund, Crosscut Ventures knows the ecosystem better than almost anyone and has a vested interest in seeing it flourish. "What's compelling is that you have an industry that is tech focused, but you also have consumers here," Maureen says. "There are so many people that are eager to start companies and build them in LA."

[Apply to]   Maureen Klewicki, info@crosscut.vc

[Links]   Web: **crosscut.vc** Twitter: **crosscutvc** LinkedIn: **company/crosscut-ventures** In:

- **Be innovative.**
  We connect with founders who are envisioning a market that's yet to be. How will your vision enable business and humans to live, excel and reach maximum potential in this world?

- **Show a clear and technical vision.**
  We seek out founders with the clear vision and focus that will bring their ideas to reality. In particular, we work with founders who take a combined technical and humanistic approach to problem-solving.

- **Have expertise.**
  We look for founders who have a personal connection to the problem they're looking to solve and who have the right capabilities, domain expertise, energy and grit to tackle it for many years to come.

- **Show intellectual honesty.**
  We value founders who are intellectually honest and approach their work with mental plasticity. The vision will evolve throughout the process, and founders need to be able to adapt with humility to grow.

[Name] # Fika Ventures

[Elevator Pitch] *"We're looking for incredible founders who are using data in an algorithmically creative way to solve meaningful problems in society."*

[Sector] **Data-driven solutions in enterprise software, fintech, digital health, marketplaces**

[Description] Fika Ventures approaches the investment process with particular empathy for entrepreneurs. Run by general partners Eva Ho and TX Zhuo, who are both former founders themselves, the investment firm is intimately familiar with the creative process of building a company from the ground up. As a B2B fund, they focus on startups offering data-driven solutions to organizations and businesses across verticals. Although Los Angeles hasn't been known for innovation in enterprise tech, the Fika team use their decades of experience in the space to provide hands-on support to companies in their portfolio. They pride themselves on their founders being their strongest references, evidence of the success of their detail-oriented and founder-supportive approach. One innovative partner company is Papaya Payments, an app that revitalizes and simplifies online payment functionality. With the app, users use their mobile device to snap a picture of an invoice (for example, a parking ticket, tax document or medical bill) and then press a button that initiates instant payment. Other companies in the Fika portfolio include Weecare, which provides a business-in-a-box for daycare providers; and Policygenius, which helps users navigate the insurance-buying process.

Fika is particularly passionate about the Los Angeles region, which Eva has witnessed growing into a bustling entrepreneurial hotspot. Bringing twenty years of experience building businesses in the city to her work at Fika Ventures, she has been excited to see the city recently emerge not just as a place for enterprises to have a small satellite office but as a veritable hub for company headquarters. She feels confident advising startups to build complex, deeptech businesses in the diverse city where founders can truly affect the lives of people from all different backgrounds and circumstances. Before cocreating Fika Ventures, Eva founded multiple companies, including Susa Ventures, and also worked at Google, while cofounder TX Zhuo worked as both a founder and at investment firms.

[Apply to] **team@fika.vc**

[Links] Web: **fika.vc** Facebook: **fikavc** Twitter: **@fikavc**

- **Have a strong founding team.**
  We prefer to fund teams with prior market and
  technology experience. We've had a lot of success with
  repeat entrepreneurs, although we fund plenty of first-
  time entrepreneurs as well.

- **Have proof of commerciality.**
  In consumer-oriented ventures, we look for highly
  engaged users. In business-oriented ventures, we look
  for revenue from at least a handful of paying customers
  who we can call and reference.

- **Have the potential to reach a large market.**
  We have to believe that a company is capable of reaching
  a $100 million–plus outcome, even if the path is uncertain
  and subject to change.

- **Incorporate internet-enabled technology.**
  Though we work with portfolio companies across
  verticals, they are typically internet enabled in
  some way. Are you creating innovation for industries
  like insurtech, fintech or healthtech? Are you using
  digital or mobile technology?

[Name]
Greycroft

[Elevator Pitch]
"Our mission is to align interests, bringing the best syndicate of investors into our portfolio companies."

[Sector]
Internet enabled

[Description]
Greycroft is a leading venture capital firm focused on investments in the internet and mobile markets. Founded in 2006, it continues to operate over a decade later as a venture fund helping companies work toward scaling. The firm, which was an early backer of Venmo and Braintree, finances companies that are in some way internet enabled. Innovations can be in mobile or digital and applied across sectors including health, insurance, food and financial technology. Though the Greycroft portfolio is diverse, its companies have in common online customer acquisition and the need for customer-acquisition strategies. With offices in two of the most important business hubs in the world – Los Angeles and New York – Greycroft is uniquely positioned to serve entrepreneurs who have chosen them as their partners. It prioritizes backing vital companies emerging from these markets and serves as a resource for enterprises looking to break into the entrepreneurial world in those regions. Greycroft leverages an extensive network of connections in the media-and-technology industry to help entrepreneurs gain visibility, build strategic relationships, bring their products to market and build successful businesses.

Greycroft manages in excess of $1 billion and has made over two hundred investments since inception. Aside from the funding itself, portfolio companies benefit from guidance in areas such as strategy and business development. They receive both access to Greycroft's network of experts and help forging connections and partnerships, as well as guidance for their eventual move towards exit. Portfolio companies that have received Greycroft investment include Scopely, a mobile-gaming business venture that uses data-platform tools to help studios launch successful video games; and App Annie, a Bay Area–based app-analytics business that provides data to app developers working in areas like financial services, airlines and ecommerce. Additional investments include Acorns, Bird, Botkeeper, Bright Health, Boxed, Braintree, Buddy Media, Everything But The House, Extreme Reach, Huffington Post, Icertis, JW Player, Maker Studios, Plated, Scopely, Shipt, TheRealReal, Thrive Market, Trunk Club, Venmo, WideOrbit and Yeahka.

[Apply to]
The best way to connect with Greycroft is through a warm introduction from angel investors or friends of the firm.

[Links]
Web: **greycroft.com** Twitter: **@greycroftvc** Instagram: **greycroftvc**

- **Focus on a new idea.**
  The most important things are: what is the problem and what is your solution? How is it different from anything else out there?

- **Start small. How big is the opportunity?**
  For us, it doesn't have to be a billion-dollar idea; it could be a $50 million- to $100 million-dollar idea that somebody else might acquire later.

- **Be an industry expert.**
  Where is the expertise on the team? Having an industry expert lets us truly know that your founding team absolutely understands the industry or area you're tackling.

- **Reach out.**
  We're great early-stage supporters of entrepreneurs in Los Angeles. For every investment, there could be twenty-five to fifty founders we sat with, gave advice to, and had follow-up emails and phone calls to answer a lot of questions for them, even if we didn't write a check.

[Name] # LDR Ventures

[Elevator Pitch] *"We're a venture capital family office that focuses on early-stage investments around consumer products and online marketplaces. We specifically focus on female and minority founders, and we're incredibly hands-on partly because our values and our team come from operational backgrounds."*

[Sector] **Consumer brands, ecommerce, technology, and marketplaces**

[Description] LDR Ventures brings something new, and critical, to venture capital: equality. By some estimates, more than two-thirds of venture capitalists are white and four in five are men. LDR Ventures was founded with the aim of evening the playing field by bringing women and founders of color into the picture and helping to guide people who have been traditionally excluded from the VC world through the process. "We're really looking to shine a spotlight on and bring attention to those who are underestimated and underappreciated," says Maxine Kozler, comanaging director for LDR Ventures.

LDR Ventures typically invests at the seed and Series A levels – a sweet spot where they can at once invest in and educate founders – with investments ranging from $100,000 to $250,000 at the seed round. The fund's first investment, a handwritten check, was a fortuitous one: Sweetgreen, the salad company, is now valued at over $1 billion. Since then, the team has invested in a number of other exciting companies. These include Court Buddies, an African American–founded company that aims to democratize access to legal services; and Thrive Market, a wholesale food startup.

In addition to capital investment, LDR Ventures sees itself as a resource that anyone in Los Angeles and other emerging markets can take advantage of. A team of interns out of Cal Poly manages the intake of pitch decks of all potential founders and makes sure everyone receives a response. For every one company that LDR Ventures invests in, the team will look at another one thousand to two thousand pitch decks, giving them advice and encouragement, if not investment. The team has made an effort to engage with communities of color in diverse cities across the country, including Miami, St. Louis and Atlanta. "We actively seek out places that don't have access to the traditional VC world," Maxine says. "We're really betting on the founder and the idea and then helping them for the rest of it."

[Apply to] **info@ldrventures.com**

[Links] Web: **ldrventures.com** LinkedIn: **company/ldr-ventures**

- **Tackle a hard problem.**
  We seek founders who are setting out to tackle
  hard problems in highly technical ways.

- **Have a unique venture.**
  We prefer to invest in new markets with few software
  competitors rather than established markets with lots
  of venture-backed competitors.

- **Be exceptional.**
  We're looking for founders who are uniquely credible
  to be building their company. We look for credibility in
  any form – technical skills, sales experience, domain
  knowledge, etc. But we always invest in founders who
  are world class at something.

- **Address the current moment.**
  Because technology moves so fast, we believe timing
  is critical when launching a startup. We want to invest
  in startups that could only be created today, not three
  years ago or three years from now.

- **Align with our vision.**
  Show us why we are the best VC firm to take
  your company to the next level.

Stage Venture Partners

[Name]

[Elevator Pitch]
"We are seed investors in software companies that are solving hard problems that matter for big enterprise customers."

[Sector]
Software technology for B2B markets

[Description]
Stage Venture Partners invests in enterprise software companies. After meeting incidentally on the board of the same nonprofit, cofounders Rob Vickery and Alex Rubalcava set out to provide early-stage funding to businesses tackling difficult problems. The firm focuses specifically on seed-stage contributions, which allows it to engage with businesses during the most creative phase of development. This specialization also means it's typically the first institutional investor, first capital and first backer of its partner companies. Stage Venture Partners eschews a specific vertical or sector designation, instead investing across fields in software applications for B2B markets. The firm does not invest in any one sector; its portfolio companies develop application software in industries as diverse as aerospace, pharmaceutical research, financial services and ecommerce. The unifying endeavor is tackling large technical problems for businesses and organizations. The harder the problem and more technical the solution, the better the fit for Stage Venture Partners.

Among the diverse companies in the firm's portfolio is VeriSIM Life. Based in San Francisco, the company aims to eliminate the need for animal testing as part of the pharmaceutical development process. Founder Jo Varshney, a trained veterinarian with a PhD in oncology, exemplifies the type of founder Stage Venture Partners seeks out: someone primed with expertise in his or her area and ready to make a huge and unique impact on a field with few competitive software incumbents. Other companies in their portfolio include Iris.TV, an AI-based video-programming platform; and Placer. ai, which provides rich foot traffic data to real estate companies.

To run Stage Venture Partners, Rob and Alex combine their own distinct backgrounds and expertise. Rob has an extensive background in international corporations, having previously worked for Lloyds Bank and Lloyds International. Alex, who previously worked at Santa Monica–based venture capital firm Anthem Venture Partners and then ran his own public equity fund, brings experience in public equity and venture capital investing.

[Apply to]
stagevp.com/contact

[Links]
Web: **stagevp.com** Facebook: **stagevp** Twitter: **@stagevp** Instagram: **stagevp**

- **Show domain/industry mastery.**
  It's vital to have a fluent understanding of the market you hope to enter. We seek founders who demonstrate expertise in their particular field.

- **Have a differentiated customer-acquisition advantage.**
  Know how you can stand out. We look for companies with a differentiated customer-acquisition strategy or the ability to identify and clearly articulate their unique distribution advantage – from other enterprises tackling a similar issue.

- **Stay focused but think big.**
  Business prowess requires short- and long-term thinking. We value entrepreneurs who can demonstrate a clear focus on a company's current needs while also maintaining a larger vision for the future.

- **Demonstrate microtraction.**
  Regardless of how early a company is, we look for founders who can demonstrate some kind of small growth trajectory.

[Name]
Wonder Ventures

[Elevator Pitch]
"We are excited to back the best founders in Los Angeles earlier than anyone else."

[Sector]
Early stage, Los Angeles based

[Description]
Wonder Ventures focuses on early-stage investment for companies in the burgeoning Los Angeles startup scene. Managing partner and founder Dustin Rosen, a former founder of a venture-backed company himself, saw a lack of financial support for LA startups in early stages – a gap that didn't exist in more developed entrepreneurial hubs like Silicon Valley. He founded Wonder Ventures to fill that space, specializing in helping companies in the first six to twelve months after initial investment to break out into their next stage of business development.

The Wonder Ventures team consists of Dustin and investment associate Abha Nath. Dustin formerly served as the CEO of Pose, one of the first consumer-shopping iPhone apps, overseeing its acquisition before leaving to start Wonder Ventures, and Abha previously worked at the Disney Accelerator and Ring. With a laser focus on investing in companies in the Los Angeles region, the firm finds its partners through a local network. It taps into university accelerator programs and encourages other founders interested in a partnership to connect through a soft introduction from a contact in the Wonder Ventures network. The Wonder Ventures team prides itself on the strong relationships they forge with founders, informed by Dustin's personal experience at the helm of a company. They value founders with a deep understanding of the industry they're entering.

One recent partner is Los Angeles startup Clutter, which, since its early days of investment, has grown to raise hundreds of millions of dollars and hire thousands of employees. The company reimagines the self-storage process, offering an alternative to those who would otherwise rent a moving truck and store items in a traditional locker. Clutter will instead come to a customer's residence, take pictures of items that need to be stored, and then take them to a twenty-four-hour secure warehouse facility. When customers need to retrieve items, they select desired items through the Clutter app, and the company then delivers them within a forty-eight-hour window.

[Apply to]
wondervc.com/contact

[Links]
Web: **wondervc.com** Twitter: **@WonderVentures**

directory

Startups

AppliedVR
1840 Century Park East,
Suite 801
Los Angeles
CA 90067
appliedvr.io

Duuple
145 S Fairfax Avenue
Los Angeles
CA 90036
duuple.com

Earny
1728 Olympic Boulevard
Santa Monica
CA 90404
earny.co

Fair
1540 2nd Street, Suite 200
Santa Monica
CA 90401
fair.com

The Female Quotient
12575 Beatrice Street
Los Angeles
CA 90066
thefemalequotient.com

NEXT Trucking
2700 East Imperial Highway
Lynwood
CA 90262
nexttrucking.com

Relativity Space
8701 Aviation Boulevard
Inglewood
CA 90301
relativityspace.com

Wondery
West Hollywood
Los Angeles, CA
wondery.com

Programs

Bixel Exchange
350 South Bixel Street
Los Angeles
CA 90017
bixelexchange.com

Grid110 Inc.
800 Wilshire Boulevard,
Suite 200
Los Angeles
CA 90017
grid110.org

MiLA
9410 Owensmouth Avenue
Chatsworth
CA 91311
makeinla.com

MuckerLab
202 Bicknell Avenue
Santa Monica
CA 90405
mucker.com

SAP Next-Gen
HanaHaus
3366 Via Lido
Newport Beach
CA 92663
sap.com/next-gen

Starburst Accelerator
840 Apollo Street, Suite 100
El Segundo
CA 90245
starburst.aero

Techstars LA
5410 Wilshire Boulevard
Los Angeles
CA 91403
techstars.com

Women Founders Network
womenfoundersnetwork.com

Spaces

CTRL Collective
12575 Beatrice Street
Los Angeles
CA 90066
ctrlcollective.com

La Kretz Innovation Campus
525 S Hewitt Street
Los Angeles
CA 90013
laincubator.org

Maker City LA
1933 South Broadway
Los Angeles
CA 90007
makercityla.com

Phase Two
5877 Obama Boulevard
Los Angeles
CA 90016
phasetwospace.com

The Riveter - Marina Del Rey
4505 South Glencoe Avenue
Marina Del Rey
CA 90292
www.theriveter.co

Toolbox LA
9410 Owensmouth Avenue
Chatsworth
CA 91311
toolbox.la

Experts

BCG Digital Ventures
1240 Rosecrans Avenue,
Suite 500
Manhattan Beach
CA 90266
bcgdv.com

DLA Piper
2000 Avenue of the Stars,
Suite 400
Los Angeles
CA 90067
dlapiper.com/en/us

Early Growth Financial Services
929 Colorado Avenue
Santa Monica
CA 90401
earlygrowthfinancialservices.com

SAP America, Inc. - Irvine
18101 Von Karman Avenue
Suite 900
Irvine
CA 92612
sap.com/next-gen

Founders

Two Bit Circus
634 Mateo Street
Los Angeles
CA 90021
twobitcircus.com

The ActOne Group
1999 W 190th St
Torrance, CA 90504
act1group.com

Enplug, Inc.
6029 Bristol Parkway,
Suite 100
Culver City
CA 90230
enplug.com

Coolhaus
8588 Washington Boulevard
Culver City
CA 90232
cool.haus

Tala
1633 26th Street
Santa Monica
CA 90404
tala.co

Schools

ArtCenter College of Design
1700 Lida Street
Pasadena
CA 91103
artcenter.edu

Cal State LA
5151 State University Drive
Los Angeles
CA 90032
calstatela.edu

Loyola Marymount University
1 LMU Drive
Los Angeles
CA 90045
lmu.edu

University of Southern California
Marshall School of Business - Bridge Hall
3670 Trousdale Pkwy
CA 90089
usc.edu

Investors

The 22 Fund
555 West 5th Street, 35th Floor
Los Angeles
CA 90013
the22fund.com

BCG Digital Ventures
1240 Rosecrans Avenue
Manhattan Beach
CA 90266
bcgdv.com

Crosscut Ventures
3402 Pico Boulevard
Santa Monica
CA 90405
crosscut.vc

Fika Ventures
1950 Sawtelle Boulevard,
Suite 183
Los Angeles
CA 90025
fika.vc

Greycroft
1375 E 6 Street, Suite 1
Los Angeles,
CA 90021
greycroft.com

LDR Ventures
2337 Roscomare Road
Los Angeles
CA 90077
ldrventures.com

Stage Venture Partners
5465 South Centinela Avenue
Los Angeles
CA 90066
stagevp.com

Wonder Ventures
wondervc.com

Event Partner

4YFN (Four Years from Now)
165 Ottley Drive
Atlanta
GA 30324
4yfn.com/los-angeles

Banks

Bank of America
888 West 7th Street, Suite 100
Los Angeles
CA 90017
fsa.merrilledge.com/willie-chang

Bank of Hope
3200 Wilshire Boulevard,
14th Floor
Los Angeles
CA 90010
bankofhope.com

Cathay Bank
777 North Broadway
Los Angeles
CA 90012
cathaybank.com

CBB Bank
3435 Wilshire Boulevard,
Suite 700
Los Angeles
CA 90010
cbb-bank.com

Citibank N.A.
Metro Southern California
Division
787 West 5th Street
Los Angeles
CA 90071
blog.citigroup.com/hello-los-angeles

City National Bank
555 South Flower Street
Los Angeles
CA 90071
cnb.com

Community Bank
460 Sierra Madre Villa
Pasadena
CA 91107
cbank.com

CTBC Bank Corp. (USA)
801 South Figueroa Street,
Suite 2300
Los Angeles
CA 90017
www.ctbcbankusa.com

East West Bank
135 North Los Robles Avenue,
7th Floor
Pasadena
Los Angeles
CA 91101
eastwestbank.com

**Farmers and Merchants Bank
of Long Beach**
302 Pine Avenue Long Beach
Los Angeles
CA 90802
fmb.com

Hanmi Bank
3660 Wilshire Boulevard,
Suite A
Los Angeles
CA 90010
hanmi.com

HSBC Bank USA, N.A.
725 South Figueroa Street
Los Angeles
CA 90017
hsbc.com

OneWest Bank
95 South Lake Avenue
Pasadena
Los Angeles
CA 91101
onewestbank.com

Pacific Premier Bank
355 South Grand Avenue, Suite
2400
Los Angeles
CA 90071
ppbi.com

Preferred Bank
601 South Figueroa Street, 29th
Floor
Los Angeles
CA 90017
preferredbank.com

Wells Fargo
333 Grand Avenue, 1st Floor
Los Angeles
CA 90071
wellsfargo.com

Coffee Shops and Places with Wifi

Andante Coffee
7623 Beverly Boulevard
Los Angeles
CA 90036
yelp.com/biz/andante-coffee-roaster-los-angeles

The Assembly
634 North Robertson Boulevard
West Hollywood
CA 90069
theassemblycafe.com

Coffee Commissary
3417 Motor Avenue
Los Angeles
CA 90034
coffeecommissary.com

Cognoscenti Coffee
1118 San Julian Street
Los Angeles
CA 90015
cogcoffee.com

Constellation Coffee
468 Foothill Boulevard, Suite B
La Cañada Flintridge
Los Angeles
CA 91011
constellationcoffeepgh.com

Document Coffee Bar
3850 Wilshire Boulevard,
Suite 107
Los Angeles
CA 90010
documentcoffeebar.com

Good Boy Bob Coffee
2058 Broadway
Santa Monica
CA 90404
goodboybob.com

Green Door Coffee
295 South Robertson Boulevard
Beverly Hills
CA 90211
greendoor.coffee

Highlight Coffee
701 East Broadway
Glendale
CA 91205
highlightcoffee.com

Hilltop Coffee + Kitchen
4427 West Slauson Avenue
Los Angeles
CA 90043
findyourhilltop.com

Ignatius Coffee
1451 Dana Street
Los Angeles
CA 90007
yelp.com/biz/ignatius-cafe-los-angeles

Mega Bodega
1001 South Broadway Avenue
Los Angeles
CA 900015
megabodegadtla.com

Patricia Coffee
108 North Alameda Street
Compton
CA 90221
patriacoffee.com/our-story.html

Rise N Grind
6501 Hollywood Boulevard
Hollywood
CA 90028
risengrindla.com

Rosebud Coffee
2302 East Colorado Boulevard
Pasadena
CA 91107
rosebudcoffee.com

Steeple House Coffee
13248 Roscoe Boulevard
Grace Community Church
Sun Valley
CA 91352
gracechurch.org/coffee

Expat Groups and Meetups

Europeans in LA
meetup.com/EuropeansinLA

Explore LA like We Don't Live Here
meetup.com/LAEvents

InterNations
internations.org

Los Angeles Startup Founder 101
meetup.com/Los-Angeles-Startup-Founder-101

Silicon Beach Young Professionals
meetup.com/siliconbeachyp/events/

Financial Services

Armanino
11766 Wilshire Boulevard,
9th Floor
Los Angeles
CA 90025
armaninollp.com

CLA
1925 Century Park East,
16th Floor
Los Angeles
CA 90067
claconnect.com

CNM
21051 Warner Center Lane,
Suite 140
Woodland Hills
Los Angeles
CA 913667
cnmllp.com

CohnReznick
1900, Avenue of the Stars, 28th Floor
Los Angeles
CA 90067
cohnreznick.com

Crowe
15233 Ventura Boulevard,
9th Floor
Sherman Oaks
Los Angeles
CA 91403
crowe.com

Deloitte
555 West 5th Street, Suite 2700
Los Angeles
CA 90013
deloitte.com

Early Growth Financial Services
929 Colorado Avenue
Santa Monica
CA 90401
earlygrowthfinancialservices.com

Ernst & Young
725 South Figueroa Street
Los Angeles
CA 90017
ey.com

Grant Thornton
515 South Flower Street,
7th Floor
Los Angeles
CA 90071
grantthornton.com

Green Hasson Janks
10990 Wilshire Boulevard,
16th Floor
Los Angeles
CA 90024
greenhassonjanks.com

Gumbiner Savett Inc.
1723 Cloverfield Boulevard
Santa Monica
Los Angeles
CA 90404
gscpa.com

Gursey Schneider
1888 Century Park East,
Suite 900
Los Angeles
CA 90067
gursey.com

Holthouse Carlin & Van Trigt
11444 West Olympic Boulevard,
11th Floor
Los Angeles
CA 90064
hcvt.com

KPMG
550 South Hope Street,
Suite 1500
Los Angeles
CA 90071
kpmg.com/us

L.A Area Chamber of Commerce
350 South Bixel Street
Los Angeles
CA 90017
lachamber.com

MGO
2029 Century Park East,
Suite 1500
Los Angeles
CA 90067
mgocpa.com

RSM US
515 South Flower Street,
17th Floor
Los Angeles
CA 90071
rsmus.com

SingerLewak
10960 Wilshire Boulevard,
7th Floor
Los Angeles
CA 90024
singerlewak.com

Flats and Rentals

Apartments
apartments.com

Forrent
forrent.com

iRoommates
iroommates.com

Kangaroom
kangaroom.com

RoomLaLa
roomlala.com

SpareRoom
spareroom.com

Trulia
trulia.com

Westside Rentals
westsiderentals.com

Zillow
zillow.com

Important Government Offices

Business Registration
City Hall, 200 N Spring Street
Los Angeles
CA 90012
finance.lacity.org

County Chief Information Office
Kenneth Hahn Hall of
Administration
500 West Temple Street Room
Los Angeles
CA 90012
lacounty.gov/chief-information-office

Department of Public Works
200 N. Spring Street, 361
Los Angeles
CA 90012-4801
dpw.lacity.org

LA Business Source Center
4311 Melrose Avenue
Los Angeles
CA 90029
business.lacity.org

Mayor's Office of Budget and Innovation
Los Angeles City Hall
200 N Spring Street
Los Angeles
CA 90012
lamayor.org/mayors-office-budget-and-innovation

Office of Extraordinary Innovation - LA Metro
Los Angeles County
Metropolitan Transportation
Authority
One Gateway Plaza
Los Angeles
CA 90012-2952
metro.net

Police Department
100 West, 1st Street
Los Angeles
CA 90012
lapdonline.org

Insurance Companies

Alliant Insurance Services, Inc.
333. South Hope Street, Suite
3750
Los Angeles
CA 90071
alliant.com/pages/default.aspx

Arroyo Insurance Services
2900 West Broadway
Los Angeles
CA 90041
arroyoins.com

Arthur J. Gallagher & Co.
505 North Brand Boulevard,
6th Floor
Glendale
Los Angeles
CA 91203
ajg.com

Bolton & Co.
3475 East Foothill Boulevard,
Suite 100
Pasadena
Los Angeles
CA 91107
boltonco.com/

Dickerson Employee Benefits
Insurance Services Inc.
1918 Riverside Drive
Los Angeles
CA 90039
dickersonbenefits.com

Hub International Insurance Services Inc.1
6701 Center Drive West, Suite
1500
Los Angeles
CA 90045
hubinternational.com/

Keenan & Associates
2355 Crenshaw Boulevard, Suite
200
Torrance
Los Angeles
CA 90501
keenan.com

Lockton Insurance Brokers
725 South Figueroa Street, 35th
Floor
Los Angeles
CA 90017
lockton.com

Poms & Associates
5700 Canoga Avenue, Suite 400
Woodland Hills
Los Angeles
CA 91367
pomsassoc.com/

SullivanCurtisMonroe
550 S.Hope Street, Suite 1000
Los Angeles
CA 90071
sullicurt.com

Total Financial & Insurance Services Inc.
300 Corporate Pointe, Suite 250
Culver City
Los Angeles
CA 90230
totalfinancial.us/

United Agencies Inc.
301 East Colorado Boulevard,
Suite 200
Pasadena
Los Angeles
CA 91101
unitedagencies.com

USI Insurance Services3
21700 Oxnard Street, Suite 1200
Woodland Hills
Los Angeles
CA 91367
usi.com

Willis Towers Watson
300 South Grand Avenue
Los Angeles
CA 90071
willistowerswatson.com

Language Schools

Adams College of English
Koreatown, Wilshire Center
3700 Wilshire Boulevard
Los Angeles
CA 90010
adamscollege.edu

Beverly Hills Lingual Institute
8383 Wilshire Boulevard, Suite 250
Beverly Hills
Los Angeles
CA 90211
bhlingual.com

California Language School
639 S New Hampshire, Suite 300
Los Angeles
CA 90005
californialanguageschool.edu

Kings Education (LA)
1555 Cassil Place
Los Angeles
CA 90028
kingseducation.com/study-locations/los-angeles

MB Language
900 North Alfred Street
Los Angeles
CA 90069
new.mblanguage.com

Mentor Language Institute
10880 Wilshire Boulevard,
Suite 122
Los Angeles
CA 90024
mliesl.edu

Pasadena Language Center
46 Smith Alley, Suite 240
Pasadena
Los Angeles
CA 91103
pasadenalanguage.com/index.html

Strommeninc
Serving Los Angeles Area
3171 Los Feliz Boulevard,
Suite 314
Los Angeles
CA 90039
strommeninc.com

TESOL Training International Los Angeles
400 Corporate Pointe
Culver City
Los Angeles
CA 90230
tesoltraining.net/?course=la

Startup Events

Adobe Max
max.adobe.com

Built in LA
builtinla.com/events

Cal/OSHA Summit 2019
store.blr.com/cal-osha-summit

Crypto Invest Summit
cis.la

Expert Dojo
expertdojo.com

Future Festival
futurefestival.com/losangeles

Hub Los Angeles
thehubla.com

LA Blockchain Week
lablockchainweek.org

MWC Los Angeles
mwclosangeles.com

Schmoozd
schmoozd.com

Startup Brunchwork with Techstars
techstars.com/startup-ecosystem-development

Summit LA
la19.summit.co

Vector
vector90.com

Women Founders Foundation
womenfoundersfoundation.org

Work Evolution
workevolution.co

glossary

A

Accelerator
An organization or program that offers advice and resources to help small businesses grow

Acqui-hire
Buying out a company based on the skills of its staff rather than its service or product

Angel Investment
Outside funding with shared ownership equity

API
Application programming interface

ARR
Accounting (or average) rate of return: calculation generated from net income of the proposed capital investment

Artificial Intelligence
The simulation of human intelligence by computer systems; machines that are able to perform tasks normally carried out by humans

B

B2B
(Business-to-Business)
The exchange of services, information and/or products from a business to a business

B2C
(Business-to-Consumer)
The exchange of services, information and/or products from a business to a consumer

Blockchain
A digital, public collection of financial accounts in which transactions made in bitcoin or another cryptocurrency are recorded chronologically

BOM
(Bill of Materials)
A list of the parts or components required to build a product

Bootstrap
To self-fund, without outside investment

Bridge Loan
A loan taken out for a short-term period, typically between two weeks and three years, until long-term financing can be organized

Burn Rate
The amount of money a startup spends

Business Angel
An experienced entrepreneur or professional who provides starting or growth capital for promising startups

Business Model Canvas
A template that gives a coherent overview of the key drivers of a business in order to bring innovation into current or new business models

C

C-level
Chief position

Cap Table
An analysis of ownership stakes in a company

CMO
Chief marketing officer

Cold-Calling
The solicitation of potential customers who had no prior interaction with the solicitor

Convertible Note/Loan
A type of short-term debt often used by seed investors to delay establishing a valuation for the startup until a later round of funding or milestone

Coworking
A shared working environment

CPA
Cost per action

CPC
Cost per click

Cybersecurity
Technologies, processes and practices designed to protect against the criminal or unauthorized use of electronic data

D

Dealflow
Term for investors that refers to the rate at which they receive potential business deals

Deeptech
Companies founded on the discoveries or innovations of technologists and scientists

Diluting
A reduction in the ownership percentage of a share of stock due to new equity shares being issued

E

Elevator Pitch
A short summary used to quickly define a product or idea

Ethereum
A blockchain-based software platform and programming language that helps developers build and publish distributed applications

Exit
A way to transition the ownership of a company to another company

F

Fintech
Financial technology

Flex Desk
Shared desk in a space where coworkers are free to move around and sit wherever they like

I

Incubator
Facility established to nurture young startup firms during their first few months or years of development

Installed Base
The number of units of a certain type of product that have been sold and are actually being used

IP
(Intellectual Property)
Property which is not tangible; the result of creativity, such as patents and copyrights

IPO
(Initial Public Offering)
The first time a company's stock is offered for sale to the public

K

KPI
(Key Performance Indicator)
A value that is measurable and demonstrates how effectively a company is achieving key business objectives

L

Later-Stage
More mature startups/companies

Lean
Refers to "lean startup methodology;" the method proposed by Eric Ries in his book for developing businesses and startups through product development cycles

Lean LaunchPad
A methodology for entrepreneurs to test and develop business models based on inquiring with and learning from customers

M

M&A
(Mergers and Acquisitions)
A merger is when two companies join to form a new company, while an acquisition is the purchase of one company by another where no new company is formed

MAU
Monthly active user

MVP
Minimum viable product

O

Opportunities Fund
Investment in companies or sectors in areas where growth opportunities are anticipated

P

P2P
(Peer-to-Peer)
A network created when two or more PCs are connected and sharing resources without going through a separate server

Pitch Deck
A short version of a business plan presenting key figures generally to investors

PR-Kit (Press Kit)
Package of promotional materials, such as pictures, logos and descriptions of a company

Product-Market Fit
When a product has created significant customer value and its best target industries have been identified

Pro-market
A market economy/ a capitalistic economy

S

SaaS
Software as a service

Scaleup
A company that has already validated its product in a market and is economically sustainable

Seed Funding
First round, small, early-stage investment from family members, friends, banks or an investor

Seed Investor
An investor focusing on the seed round

Seed Round
The first round of funding

Series A/B/C/D
The name of funding rounds that come after the seed stage

Shares
Units of ownership of a company that belong to a shareholder

Solopreneurs
A person who sets up and runs a business on their own and typically does not hire employees

Startup
Companies under three years old, in the growth stage and becoming profitable (if not already)

SVP
Senior Vice President

T

Term Sheet/Letter of Intent
The document between an investor and a startup including the conditions for financing (commonly non-binding)

U

Unicorn
A company often in the tech or software sector worth over US$1 billion

USP
Unique selling point

UX
(User experience design) The process of designing and improving user satisfaction with products so that they are useful, easy to use and pleasurable to interact with

V

VC
(Venture Capital) Financing from a pool of investors in a venture capital firm in return for equity

Vesting
Process that involves giving or earning a right to a present or future payment, benefit or asset

Z

Zebras
Companies which aim for sustainable prosperity and are powered by people who work together to create change beyond a positive financial return

Traction Ave - Los Angeles

STARTUP GUIDE *NORDICS*   The Entrepreneur's Handbook

STARTUP GUIDE *JOHANNESBURG*   The Entrepreneur's Handbook

STARTUP GUIDE *TRONDHEIM*   The Entrepreneur's Handbook

STARTUP GUIDE *HAMBURG*   The Entrepreneur's Handbook

STARTUP GUIDE *CAPE TOWN*   The Entrepreneur's Handbook

STARTUP GUIDE *LUXEMBOURG*   The Entrepreneur's Handbook

STARTUP GUIDE *VIENNA*   The Entrepreneur's Handbook

STARTUP GUIDE *TEL AVIV*   The Entrepreneur's Handbook

STARTUP GUIDE *MADRID*   The Entrepreneur's Handbook

STARTUP GUIDE *VALENCIA*   The Entrepreneur's Handbook

STARTUP GUIDE *COPENHAGEN*   The Entrepreneur's Handbook

STARTUP GUIDE *PARIS*   The Entrepreneur's Handbook

STARTUP GUIDE *REYKJAVIK*   The Entrepreneur's Handbook

STARTUP GUIDE *LOS ANGELES*   The Entrepreneur's Handbook

STARTUP GUIDE *STOCKHOLM*   The Entrepreneur's Handbook

STARTUP GUIDE *MUNICH*   The Entrepreneur's Handbook

STARTUP GUIDE *FRANKFURT*   The Entrepreneur's Handbook

STARTUP GUIDE *ZURICH*   The Entrepreneur's Handbook

STARTUP GUIDE *LONDON*   The Entrepreneur's Handbook

STARTUP GUIDE *LISBON*   The Entrepreneur's Handbook

STARTUP GUIDE *SINGAPORE*   The Entrepreneur's Handbook

STARTUP GUIDE *NEW YORK*   The Entrepreneur's Handbook

STARTUP GUIDE *BERLIN*   The Entrepreneur's Handbook

STARTUP GUIDE *OSLO*   The Entrepreneur's Handbook

STARTUP GUIDE *CAIRO*   The Entrepreneur's Handbook

→ startupguide.com   Follow us

About the Guide

Based on traditional guidebooks that can be carried around everywhere, Startup Guide books help you navigate and connect with different startup scenes across the globe. Each book is packed with useful information, exciting entrepreneur stories and insightful interviews with local experts. Today, Startup Guide books are in two dozen cities in Europe, Asia, the US and the Middle East, including Berlin, London, Singapore, New York and Tel Aviv. As part of our partnership with One Tree Planted, each book we sell contributes toward the planting of a tree.

How we make the guides:

To ensure an accurate and trustworthy guide every time, we team up with local partners that are established in their respective startup scene. We then ask the local community to nominate startups, coworking spaces, founders, schools, investors, incubators and established businesses to be featured through an online submission form. Based on the results, these submissions are narrowed down to the top hundred organizations and individuals. Next, the local advisory board – which is selected by our community partners and consists of key players in the local startup community – votes for the final selection, ensuring a balanced representation of industries and startup stories in each book. The local community partners then work in close collaboration with our international editorial and design team to help research, organize interviews with journalists as well as plan photoshoots with photographers. Finally, all content is reviewed, edited and put into the book's layout by the Startup Guide team in Berlin and Lisbon before going for print in Berlin.

Where to find us: The easiest way to get your hands on a Startup Guide book is to order it from our online shop: startupguide.com/books

If you prefer to do things in real life, drop by one of the fine retailers listed on the stockists page on our website.

Want to become a stockist or suggest a store?

Get in touch here:
sales@startupguide.com

The Startup Guide Stores

Whether it's sniffing freshly printed books or holding an innovative product, we're huge fans of physical experiences. That's why we have stores in Berlin, Lisbon and Copenhagen. Not only do the stores showcase our books and a range of curated products, they're also our offices and a place for the community to come together and share wows and hows. But our stores wouldn't be possible without the help of Toyno, an experience design studio based in Lisbon. Visit their website here: toyno.com.

Lisbon:
Rua do Grilo 135, 1950-144 Lisboa, Portugal
Mon-Fri: 10h-18h
+351 21 139 8791
lisbon@startupguide.com

Berlin:
Maybachufer 6, 12047 Berlin, Germany
Mon-Fri: 10h-18h
+49 30 21 60 06 62
berlin@startupguide.com

Copenhagen:
Borgbjergsvej 1, 2450 København, Denmark
Mon-Fri: 9h-16h
+45 51 79 19 58
copenhagen@startupguide.com

#startupeverywhere

Startup Guide was founded by Sissel Hansen in 2014. As a publishing and media company, we produce guidebooks and online content to help entrepreneurs navigate and connect with different startup scenes across the globe. As the world of work changes, our mission is to guide, empower and inspire people to start their own business anywhere. Today, Startup Guide books are in two dozen cities in Europe, Asia, the US and the Middle East, including London, Stockholm, Vienna, Paris, Singapore, New York, Miami and Tel Aviv. We also have three physical stores in Berlin, Lisbon and Copenhagen which double as offices for our 20-person team. Visit our website for more: startupguide.com

Want to get more info, be a partner or say hello?

Shoot us an email here: info@startupguide.com

Join us and #startupeverywhere

City Advisory Board

Ann Rosenberg
Senior Vice President
of UN Partnerships
and Global Head of
SAP Next-Gen
SAP

Allison Beck
Director of Marketing
and Business
Development
Greycroft

Andy Wilson
Executive Director
The Alliance for
SoCal Innovation

Aria Safar
Economic Policy
Manager
Office of Los Angeles
Mayor Eric Garcetti

Ben Christensen
Global Innovation
Manager at SAP
Next-Gen and
Science Fiction
Community Lead
SAP

Billy O'Grady
Senior Vice President
City National Bank

**Chandra
Subramaniam**
Dean, David Nazarian
College of Business
and Economics
California State
University Northridge

Chris Manriquez
Vice President
for Information
Technology/CIO
California State
University,
Dominguez Hills

Chris Rico
Director of Innovation
+ Digital Media
& Entertainment
Industry Cluster
Development
Los Angeles
County Economic
Development
Corporation

Darlene Fukuji
Assistant Director,
Fred Kiesner Center
for Entrepreneurship
Loyola Marymount
University

Dustin Rosen
Managing Partner
Wonder Ventures

Fred Farina
Chief Innovation
and Corporate
Partnerships Officer
Caltech

Hovig Tchalian
Faculty in
Entrepreneurship
Drucker School
of Management,
Claremont Graduate
University

John Diep
Founder, CEO
Schmoozd

Jose Gomez
Executive VP and
Chief Operating
Officer
Cal State LA

Juan Vasquez
Data Programs
Manager
City of Los Angeles
Office
of Finance

Kerry Bennett
Head of Marketing
Upfront Ventures

Kevin Winston
CEO & Founder
Digital LA

Krisztina 'Z' Holly
Host, The Art of
Manufacturing
podcast
Founder & Chief
Instigator,
MAKE IT IN LA

Maureen Klewicki
Senior Associate
Crosscut Ventures

Michael Kelly
Executive Director
The Los Angeles
Coalition for the
Economy & Jobs

Mike Swords
VP Government
Affairs and
International
Relations
Los Angeles
Cleantech Incubator

Miki Reynolds
Cofounder &
Executive Director
Grid110

Niles Friedman
Strategic Advisor
Los Angeles County

Sandra Moerch
Chief Content
Director
at SAP Next-Gen
SAP

Tara Roth
President
Goldhirsh Foundation

**Yolanda 'Cookie'
Parker**
Board Member
Yes2Jobs

With thanks to our **Content Partners**

And our **Event Partners**

4YFN | Connecting **Startups**

With thanks to our **Community Partner**

The Los Angeles Coalition
A COALITION FOR THE ECONOMY & JOBS IN LOS ANGELES

Event Partner
/ 4YFN Los Angeles

4YFN (4 Years from Now) is one of the world's most influential startup business platforms enabling startups, investors and corporations to create, discover and launch new ventures together. Held alongside MWC, the leading business event for the mobile industry, 4YFN is the forum for entrepreneurship. Technology is changing the world, but entrepreneurs are changing technology.

Hosted within MWC19 on October 22–24 at the Los Angeles Convention Center, the second edition of 4YFN promises a fresh pipeline for investment opportunities and lead generation. It is the younger, more fun side of the tech industry – more boisterous and less mature.

The focus of 4YFN's mission is startups, helping them to learn, connect and grow within the technology ecosystem. As part of MWC, 4YFN benefits from its strong connections to major corporate players and investors who head to 4YFN looking for products and services to commercialize. For others, it is a place to network and evangelize – or just to find some transcendently cool innovations.

This year there will be over 150 startups exhibiting, and they will be outnumbered by investors and leading corporate innovation partners. The event program will include celebrity and inspirational keynote talks, book launches, onstage panels and fireside chats curated by leading entrepreneurial experts. 4YFN will inaugurate its successful Discovery Area from 4YFN Barcelona for the first time in LA, which includes the 4YFN Investors and Community Clubs, a dedicated area for workshops and mentorships, and a non-stop pitching stage.

4YFN will also launch an Investor Festival, in partnership with Expert Dojo, which will facilitate over five hundred one-on-one investor/entrepreneur speed-pitching meetings.

WHERE NEXT?